CW00405849

Maurice Perkins book synops

A true story of life in Greater Manchester through the sixties and seventies that pushed a boy to become a man in the Royal Navy.

Armed Forces experiences that catapulted his development and forged bonds with comrades who became friends for life and the lessons learned that he took with him into civilian life.

The story is told in a humorous and gritty style, describing events and incidents, fast paced and straight from the heart. Mostly funny, there is a sober and occasional sad side to the events, which match the ups and downs of life.

Maurice describes himself as a Scallywag who became an Executive. Never slow in expressing himself, he paints a picture of life that is not always visible to everyone.

Preface

Conversation, verbal exchanges, providing and responding to oral instructions are all a daily part of life and something I have always enjoyed. Having a laugh when I can, ensuring that people understand or that I understand what is needed and what is going on. However, it has been noted, many, many times, by many people, that I can be a bit lippy.......

So what does being a bit lippy mean. Seeing the funny side of things when others cannot but speaking out anyway, ad-libs, swift responses, that sort of thing. I can quip with the best and am easily disappointed with the opposite, which I call "slopes" or slow responses. Where someone has to really think to say something remotely witty. Me, I can throw them off the cuff with the best of people.

However, quips have got me into lots of different types of trouble over the years, including having my head kicked in (literally), falling out with friends and family, resorting to fisticuffs (many times) or reducing a sombre business gathering into fits of laughter. I like to make people laugh.

All of these accounts are based on real events, involving real people and recollected from my perspectives. No harm is intended, other than to inform our social history and make people smile. I hope you enjoy the read...

Maurice Perkins

aka Moz, aka Polly, aka Mo

Book Two of Two

Synopsis

Preface

Glossary of terms

Born in Stockport - Grew up in the Royal Navy

Born in Stockport - Grew up in the Royal Navy

Glossary of Terms

AB	Able Rate / Able Seaman
Bobbins	Rubbish
Bootneck, or Bootie	Royal Marine
Crabfat	Airman
Dabtoe	Seaman
Dhoby	Wash or Clean
Fag	Cigarette
Gash	Rubbish
Gopher	Big Wave
Guzz	Plymouth
Hank Marvin, or just Hank	Starving (hungry)
HMS	Her Majesties Ship
Hooky	Leading Rate / Leading Hand
Joss	Master At Arms, chief of naval police
Matelot	Sailor
Mither	Continually harangue
NAAFI	Navy Army Air Force Institute
Oggin	The Sea
Oppo	Close friend, mate, opposite number
Pompey	Portsmouth
Pongo	Soldier
POTS	Petty Officer Telegraphist
RA	Ration Allowance (for stating in civilian accommodation)
RS	Radio Supervisor (Petty Officer)
Scablifter	Naval medic
Scallywag	Street urchin, trouble causer, thug
Slate	Amount of debt owed
The mob	HM Armed Forces
Vet	Naval medic
WAFU	Fleet Air Arm – Wet And Fucking Useless
Zed's	Sleep zzzzzz

Born in Stockport - Grew up in the Royal Navy

Born in Stockport - Grew up in the Royal Navy

Opening Chapter

How did I get to here?

The first book covers this period in my life in far more detail, however, in summary, I was born into a loving family who had limited resources. My parents made lots of sacrifices to improve themselves and our family. They gave us a love of creativity, respect for one and another and the gift of sharing. Whatever we have, no matter how little, we can always share it with our family and our friends.

Mum and Dad started off in a two-up, two-down terraced house that fronted onto the street and had a small backyard. It was demolished in the big slum clearances of the 1960's but by then we had moved to slightly higher quality of council house.

My school career was not outstanding, though I peaked in year one and two of high school and won an award for top of the year, before succumbing to the teenage ailment of thumbing my nose at the world and becoming a scallywag.

Whilst there are clear trigger points of events and decisions, all told in a candid manner and with some humour, those incidents themselves have been major learning points for me and my own family.

The Royal Navy was my saviour in many ways, without that constant drive to improve, to learn and deal with the challenges of being part of Her Majesties Armed Forces, there is doubt that I would have been as much of a success as I have.

There is also no doubt that being able to see the funnier side of things has made my life an interesting kaleidoscope and one that I have no hesitation in sharing with others. To inform and to amuse.

Having joined the Royal Navy in 1974, signed on the dotted line and swore my allegiance to Queen and Country, I fell into a world that was so radically different from anything that I had experienced in my youth.

Born in Stockport - Grew up in the Royal Navy

I sailed through basic training and received awards for my purpose and delivery. A junior class leader and a quick learner, I soon found myself in positions of responsibility at quite a young age.

I also failed to master the appropriate control of alcohol intake, a matter which will surface on a regular basis and foundation for many escapades and adventures.

Please read on...

Chapter Two

HMS Ambuscade

I got the train down to Guzz and met my new shipmates the day we sailed. As I got on there was a pipe to clear lower deck and RV in the dining hall. I left my kit with the Quarter Master and I clambered down the ladders to the dining hall.

I stood at the back of the crowd whilst the Executive Officer (XO) or Number One, briefed the ships company on the forthcoming tour to an enemy port!

Shocked, as I had looked at the itinerary before I left Pompey and as far as I could see we weren't down to visit any soviet pact bases or anything similar, as the XO continued with his briefing.

The French have been our enemy since the bastards invaded us in 1066 and I don't want any of you bringing the Royal Navy into disrepute. Try keep the fighting to the back streets where you can and don't get arrested…. What an introduction.

The communicators were billeted with the chefs, stewards and storemen in 2D mess, nicknamed the Picnic Club. It didn't take long to work out why. We got all sorts of tit bits from the galley and stuff that had been destined for the wardroom but found its way down to the Picnic Club. There was always a bit of a buffet or cakes in the mess. Lovely.

Our first visit was to the French naval base at Brest. Anyone knowing their WW2 history will recall that we bombed Brest mercilessly throughout the war as it was the home to a large fleet of German submarines that were terrorising the Atlantic convoys, so desperately needed to keep the UK fed.

The fact we were there to commemorate the Battle of the Atlantic seemed somehow lost on our French hosts. It kicked off everywhere.

I turned out for the Ambuscade's second team in a game against the second team of our host vessel the FS Kersaint. An absolute horror of a game.

The pitch was ringed by French sailors and every time a brit matelot got anywhere near the touchline they were tripped up, barged or punched from the spectators. Throw-ins and corners were a lottery as to how much punishment you would take. Gibbo, a big scruffy steward from Bolton could play a bit. He was also a dirty bastard and told us to slide into the spectators if we got the chance and take a few out. So that's what we did. I think we lost the match but crippled a few in the crowd as well as some of the opposition players.

The post-match necessity of hosting us was a perfunctory affair with a small beer and a microscopic slice of a cheese and ham crusty bread was handed to us queueing up at a dining hall hatch. Then we were hurried to drink and eat up and fuck off out of their club. Which we did.

That evening it was carnage all over Brest as we scrapped with the French in bars, in side streets. Two of our lads were mugged by a French taxi driver for fucks sake. Lots of arrests, lots of injuries but I think we acquitted ourselves well enough for a ships company of about 175 and we did okay. I remember being in one bar and we were all drinking bottles of wine (bottle each) and glugging from the bottle.

The guy that owned the bar was in raptures of how much stuff we were buying and putting away. Then it kicked off outside and so he locked us in to protect us and probably protect his revenue. When we were ready to leave, he arranged for us to exit through the back so we could avoid the pitched battle and the police out the front. Good man.

The Type-21 frigates were a new build design using the latest lightweight materials, less than average armament but powered by Rolls Royce

Olympus gas turbine engines that gave them a pretty good top speed of 32 knots, or 37mph. However, as a number of my colleagues were to discover to their peril, the lightweight construction materials were pretty shit and exposed when the ships saw action in the Falklands in 1982.

In my haste to depart Pompey and leave the sexually adventurous Margaret to her own devices I had left my prized possessions there. Three scrapbooks of photographs from when I was a kid until I joined the Antrim, along with a small box of northern soul and Motown singles (45rpm records) and they were still there.

I was in regular correspondence with my mates on the Antrim and they kept me posted on how the football team was progressing and who was shagging which barmaid etc. Gordon "Gabby" Hayes my Bolton mukka wrote to me most, along with Frank (the bottle) a dry humoured bunting from Barnsley. I desperately wanted my photo albums and limited-edition records back.

Frank took up the cudgel as his bird, a nurse called Amy, had a car. Always a bonus to trap a bird with a car, it meant you could get out to country pubs and not the endless matelot filled bars in town. Anyway, I think Frank had Debbie and another mate, Andy Croxton from Stoke with him. They went round to her house but she wasn't in, just her brother, who refused them entry. Undeterred, they rushed him at the door and went in and up to her bedroom, with him shouting that he was going to call the police. He didn't.

They got my albums and singles box and took them away to the safety of their own digs. However, when I returned to UK and could get down to Pompey in the new year of 1979 to take possession. She had lifted a number of my rare northern soul records and took 5 photographs from my albums. All photographs of my little brother Ged. Bizarre. That was the end of anything I had to do with her. Apart from when Gabby wrote to me.

Gabby was a regular "corresponder" so it was no surprise to read about how well the mess football team was doing, now they all had proper boots and all. How the refit was going and other stuff, then we got to the meaty bit on page three. Sorry mate, in a drunken moment at a party, I shagged Margaret.

I wrote back to Hayes with a chirpy message of how I had dumped Margaret before we sailed on the Ambuscade and a week later he responded with another letter explaining that it wasn't just him that had shagged Margaret, there were four of them in a line taking turns. What a girl. God knows whatever happened to her. A nymphomaniac, kleptomaniac and pathological liar. Probably a psychologist's wet dream somewhere.

I had been drafted onto the Ambuscade to lead a watch. There was some resistance from at least one lad onboard who thought it should have been him but it wasn't, it was me and we had a pretty candid conversation about it and no trouble.

After a few weeks, the SCO pulled me to one side and complimented me on my hard work, how I had got to grips with the satellite communications (known as SCOT) and one of only two people who could re-tune it when it went out of synchronisation, which was often and usually when we were anchored up somewhere. Anyway, he wanted to congratulate me on how I handled things and said he wanted to draft CW papers on me. Wow. I was staggered.

CW papers meant Commission Warrant. Wow scabby ab Moz Perkins an officer. I couldn't see it myself so I asked him whether he had read my personal docs and he admitted that he hadn't received them yet. Paperwork always travelled slowly in the mob. I suggested that he wait until he had read my docs and then maybe we could have another chat. He thought that would be a sensible approach and we left it there.

It was a month or so later that my personal document package arrived. Probably slightly heavier than the normal able rate I guess with all the trouble I had been in. His face when he broached the subject again with me was a picture. He couldn't weigh up the person he had come to know and the litany of events my personal file contained.

We agreed that drafting CW papers was probably not a good idea right now but maybe on another occasion. Yes, like another ship, or another career maybe. Ha ha but not the first time that an officer wanted to me to be commissioned.

With my experience as a cartoonist, I picked up the cudgel with others to run the ships newspaper, The Pistol Post and worked closely with my good friend Luigi (Victor Cox) a chunky funny scot who could play guitar, sing and could write funny poems. We had a lot of fun together doing it.

We had a good trip over to the States, working hard with the US Navy on a number of major exercises, a great skipper and a strong character of an XO made us a pretty good fighting unit. I had also signed up for IS duties and regularly drilled with an SLR. We almost got to be used in action during some form of uprising on one of the Caribbean islands when the Governor was held ransom for something. We steamed at speed to get there and all got kitted out ready to be deployed but it was all over by the time we got there. Never mind.

Stopping off in Cartegena, Columbia was a ball. Typical routine when a warship visits a foreign port, an officer is despatched a week before to gen up on what's what. He returns with maps of the area's matelots should not go to as they are dangerous. All this serves to do is provide jack with a list of places to visit and things to must do while you are there and Cartegena was no different. A red-light district that I surmise was controlled by the drug barons but all that was above my level of understanding at that point, it was just full of lovely ladies and cheap beer. Therefore. a magnet for matelots.

There was a club called the "Las Velas Bar". It was massive and full of scantily dressed pretty young girls and every single one of them a lady of the night. I had made a vow to myself, never to pay for sex but sat in the bar on the first evening with a girl straddling my lap and gently moving up and down and two other girls, one each side, groping, stroking and kissing me, I have to say my resolve was tested. I was that hard I could have broken a plate with it.

The girl on my lap looked like a young Martha Reeves of the Vandellas fame and I thought right. Let's do it. So off we went as my mates behind me cheered me on. She led me through the crowd to a different part of the club, separated by a wrought iron fence that ran floor to ceiling and wall to wall, with the one gate guarded by a guy with a sub-machine gun…

I have to say, I was a little disconcerted as he nodded us through and towards a staircase with another guy sat down with a shotgun across his thighs who also acknowledged me with a nod. I felt even less confident as we got up the stairs to a first-floor landing with a number of doors off it and yet another gun toting chap who nodded to me as though he knew me and off down the corridor we went, with less vigour being demonstrated in my skidders.

She opened the door to a cramped and smelly little room containing a concrete divan with a thin mattress on it, a dirty sheet and red plastic bucket in the corner containing a murky liquid. She closed the door behind me, then whipped off her frock with one movement to reveal a lithe brown figure that under normal circumstances would have been difficult to avoid.

However, all the romance in the air ended as she squatted over the red plastic bucket and used one hand to splash the murky water up and around her parts in what was probably a visual indication she was now cleaned out and ready for me. I properly deflated and as my cock retreated into a defensive position I had only two thoughts.

The first was a definite one. In no way on earth was I going to shove my willy into that under no circumstances whatsoever, not in this lifetime or any other. It was a "Nil Pwa" as far I was concerned. No. definitely not. The second was an expression of concern about how the hell I was going to get out of here and past all the men with guns.

She beckoned me onto the smelly bed and still trying to work things out in my head, I did. Her English was no better than my non-existent Spanish and she was clearly getting a bit upset but I did enough with my visual signalling that sex was a non-starter but that I was happy giving her the three quid's worth of klebbies for the experience.

She rubbed up against me and gyrated for the time it took to smoke a fag and I thought yep, that's about long enough for a shag and we got dressed. We held hands and made our way along the corridor, down the stairs and through the gates passed all the gun toting and nodding amigo's until we got back to the masses of dancing and beer swilling matelots and I felt a tad safer.

I arrived to meet my mess mates who all cheered and demonstrated that male signal that successful copulation has taken place by raising a fisted arm and slapping a hand across the elbow. For fucks sake. Yeh! But of course, I hadn't and that was my story to tell on another day but not then.

We sailed from Cartegena and there was the usual queue outside the Vets office having their bits checked out and carry out urine tests to see if anything had gone awry in Columbia. We called the scablifter Medical Assistants Vets because someone once read in a dictionary that a Vet was a medically trained person not competent to treat human beings. Which is how we saw them.

That evening we had a senior visitor into the MCO. The officer responsible for our scablifter. He wasn't a medically trained officer, but someone who had done a 4-week course at RN Hospital Haslar which probably qualified him to be a brain surgeon or something. Anyway, he demands that we set up the off-line enciphering kit as he has a Medical-In-Confidence urgent signal to send.

The off-line encipher was a piece of kit based on the Enigma machine created by the Germans in WW2, although with some extra refinements. We had to set up each rotor and the officer had a couple of tweaks he could add out of our sight. He would set it up and then type away creating a steady stream of five letter groups. We then formed the groups into a message that was despatched to whoever he wanted it to. In this case MODUK and the US Naval Base we were due to arrive in at Long Beach in California.

When he finished, he switched the machine off and left us to break it back down. They used to be lazy and thought that once they had switched it off, it would scramble the rotors. That would have been so had he taken the moment to un-tweak his element of the rotors. In my experience, most officers were generally lazy and just switched it off and would walk out.

A radio operator will then switch on the cypher kit and type in the five-letter groups until the message comes out. That way, we always knew what was going on.

What was going on was a shock. Of a ships company of 175 souls, the Vet had carried out urine tests and discovered 85 sailors had a dose. This would be too much for his limited stock of penicillin and the signal was requesting support from the US Navy.

I started itching down below. At first I thought it was a bit of "dhoby rash" created when handwashing underwear and failing to rinse out the soap suds sufficiently. Then when you sweat, it reacts with the soap and causes a nasty itchy rash.

After the three days of being incredibly itchy, in and around the groin, my armpits started itching. Therefore, not dhoby rash. I went to see the vet, who confirmed it was crabs. Brilliant. Take this pungent and caustic cream. Rub it all over your body where you have hair, paying particular attention to your groin of course. Wait a spell, then shower it off. Throw away your towel, your flannel and buy new underwear. Great.

I asked him not to tell the boys in the mess and could we keep it between the two of us. Relying heavily on the Hippocratic Oath, though I realised shortly afterwards, he must have failed to sign it.

Entering the mess, I was received with cries of "Unclean!" and mock bell-ringing with everyone avoiding me as if the crabs could jump three feet or more. Maybe they can. I didn't know.

I stripped off and started the task of getting the grey goo rubbed in. I couldn't reach my hairy back and asked my oppo Tom Bowler, a Dusty and real name Ian. To help. He just fucked off. Cheers mate. But he did come back wearing elbow length rubber gloves from stores and rubbed the cream into my back at arm's length.

Born in Stockport - Grew up in the Royal Navy

Waiting until my skin started to tingle as the caustic elements of the cream started to work, I completed the task of bagging up all my skidders and headed off to the bathroom with my towel and flannel to wash off the gunk.

I then ditched the towel and flannel and made do for a day or so until I could buy a new towel and underwear. Reducing the number of beer chits I had left.

Passing through the Panama Canal was an experience that took all day. A tad boring if truth be known but then we were in the Pacific and worked with another load of US Navy ships on more exercises along with visiting some beautiful places. However, first we had to berth in Long Beach and to the surprise of the entire ships company, except for the wardroom and communicators, a mobile hospital was being craned into place on the jetty.

All the boys who had a dose had stoppage of leave until they had received the correct amount of penicillin. This cramped the style of a lot of people. We were all given a one-week "station leave" pass and some of us had decided to hire a car and drive to Las Vegas. Some who were supposed to come with us in a small cavalcade didn't and had to remain behind.

We hired a Ford Pinto, well Dave Eaton did, a laid-back lad from Timperley in Cheshire and a bunting. Never any urgency with Dave, he was the only one of the five us to be over 21 and had the ID to prove it. Polly Perks a steward, Bungy Williams a writer, Pete Atwell our radio electrical mechanic and yours truly commenced our trip to Vegas the following day.

After all of the 85 matelots locked back on board were tested and waited days for the results, they were diagnosed as 11 cases of VD and 74 bladder infections. The Vet did a runner. However, we didn't find any of that out until we returned over a week later. We were on a road trip. 300 miles or so to Vegas Baby!

Born in Stockport - Grew up in the Royal Navy

We agreed to share the driving and had a bit of a rota. All seemed to be going well as we drove along Interstate 15, with occasional stops at diners for food and piss-stop. Then at some point short of halfway to Vegas we could detect a burning smell in the car. It got worse until we thought we had better stop and take a look.

Although the car mechanic knowledge amongst the five of us totalled exactly zero, we lifted the hood to take a look. However, despite our lack of knowledge, we could all see a bit of the engine glowing white hot and watched as it cooled down to red hot and then eventually after an hour so it cooled right down. At which point we thought it was okay to drive on. Except the car wouldn't. Start, that is.

Looking forward up the road, the highway just vanished into the horizon and it was the same looking back. Like that movie "Vanishing Point". Dave said he thought we had passed a sign behind us and so walked back. We did try to flag some cars and lorries down to ask for assistance but all motored past, some beeped their horns but no-one stopped.

Dave returned and said, the sign showed a town just a mile away called Barstow. So, we did the looking forward thing again but could only see the road to the horizon. Pete and I said we would jog forward and check it out. So, we did.

Born in Stockport - Grew up in the Royal Navy

WHITING MOTELS - W. BARSTOW, CALIFORNIA

As we jogged forward a valley started to appear and the road was elevated to bridge the divide and one reason why the optical illusion showed horizon as all the land around as dusty. So, we jogged back and with no other alternative, decided to push the car. It wasn't easy in the dying heat of the evening but we changed driver around for a rest and kept plugging away until we reached the off-ramp. Where we all jumped in and freewheeled down the ramp and straight into the car park of a motel and pulled up.

Dave found a call box and spoke to the hire company who said it would take some time to sort out a repair so we were stranded for now in this little town of Barstow. Eager to make the best of it, we checked into the motel and got a room with two king sized beds and a cot. Bungy as the smallest got the cot and the rest of bunked two by two.

We got showered, shaved and put on our best to go out on the town. The motel manager said that the nearest bar was less than a mile away, which we thought was an easy walk and set off en-masse. We hadn't got more than a few hundred yards when a "whoop whoop" sounded as a police car pulled alongside us and the cop challenged us to what we were doing. So, we told him. The car had broken down and we are stuck here, so just walking to the bar. He explained that nobody walked anywhere in America and so gave us all a lift into town and deposited us at the first bar. We thanked him and went in for our first US beer. Or not.

The bar staff challenged us for ID and knowing the rule was only 21 and over got served, we waffled that we were on holiday and had left our passports in the motel safe. Okay they said, just go back and get it and we can serve you. This was repeated in the next three bars we walked into and required an immediate and drastic solution.

Born in Stockport - Grew up in the Royal Navy

We went into a drug store and bought a packet of loose razor blades. Spent some time cutting between the laminated sheets of our RN ID cards to carefully prise out the bit of card depicting our dates of birth, gently scrubbed them out and inserted the year 1956 on each of them therefore instantly turning us in to 21-year-olds. Lick and press the pieces back into place. Problem solved.

The very next bar we walked into was the Holiday Inn and they assumed we were residents and never asked us for our ID. Ha ha ha. Still the doctored ID cards would come into their own when we returned to Long Beach and went drinking in Los Angeles.

We got stuck into some cold beer and started to enjoy the old boy playing western songs on his guitar and then became the entertainment by singing along with him. More so when he said if we sang some more he would buy us some more. Free beers. Hey magic. So, we did.

It created a bit of a party atmosphere in the bar and we egged everyone on to join us. Some women came over to us and dragged us over to their tables with their husbands and boyfriends etc. they were all Marine Instructors playing in a military soft ball tournament in Barstow. We had a cracking time. The party then moved on to our motel room and we invited everyone to join us. The bar staff, the doormen and the Marines and their partners.

In turn, the Marines invited us to join them at the military base the following day to watch them play softball. So, we did.

Four days of non-stop drinking and being the mascots of the Marine Corps Recruitment Depot, San Diego with all the evening parties commencing in the Holiday Inn and then carrying forward into more drinking and cavorting in our motel room. It was epic.

On the third morning the motel manager knocked on the door and said we had to move. So sheepishly we packed up our bags and trudged out but she said not out, out. Just out to another room so I can give this one a heavy clean. Hurray. So, we invited her and her husband to all the remaining parties. I only have a limited memory of events but there was a lot of shagging, balancing antics on the roof and endless drinking.

Born in Stockport - Grew up in the Royal Navy

Our routine was to get a cab to the liquor store mid-morning once vision was temporarily resumed and stock up on bottles of Boones Farm Strawberry Hill Original Wine, cans of beer and bags of ice. Then return to the motel room and fill our two large waste bins with the alcohol and stuff ice all round them, before getting a cab to the military base outside the town.

There the Marines filled us up all day with beer whilst we heckled the opposition. Endlessly. No fisticuffs because we were protected by some of the biggest musclemen I had ever seen from the MCRD and their wives, some of whom were just animals.

The evening RV was the Holiday Inn and the cycle continued. The car got fixed but MCRD had got into the final, so we stayed another night in Barstow so we could watch them win the tournament for the first time and they said it was all down to the English navy guys who were their mascots.

The yanks never seem to recognise the Royal Navy as being anything other than English. Something that always made me smile and wound up the provincials from Scotland, Wales and Northern Ireland.

Then we drove on to Vegas. Via stops at Lake Mead and a western ghost town for photos. We got a less than plush motel on the strip in Vegas.

Expensive for what it was and for just our last two nights, Friday and Saturday before we had to return to the ship.

Vegas was strangely lower key to Barstow and I know that may seem daft to say but that's how it felt. Vegas is just a machine to make money for the people who provide the entertainment. It's cold and calculating and no matter how hard we tried, we couldn't generate the same atmosphere. Sure, we did a few casino's and bet on the things we understood and watched craps being played without ever understanding the rules of the game properly.

Spent up, we exited the hotel Sunday afternoon for a drive west back to Long Beach and it was a bit of a haul. Hungry, we decided to stop en-route for a break and decided to make that in Barstow again but we hardly had any money left. We were literally brassic. When Bungy said he thought he had heard some shrapnel rolling about under the back seat and we should investigate. So, we did.

We ripped up the seat and broke part of its mounting and found a treasure chest underneath. Granted it was quarters, nickels and dimes but there was oodles of it. There was also a lot of shit in with it, so it took a while to get it all sorted out. That with the remnants of our kitty and what was in our pockets came to about $25 and we knew we could at least get a burger and a beer each. So, we headed off to the Holiday Inn.

We were a bit embarrassed to think we would drop a massive handful of coins on the bar and order a burger and a beer each but the end justifies the means and we were going to front it out. What met us was just incredulous. The doormen split up, one to rush inside to tell the bar staff and the other to welcome us back and wave us into a parking spot.

Ushered into the bar, we never had to put a hand in our pockets as the staff and some of the customers continued to buy us drinks for the rest of the evening until the bar shut at 2am and they lamented that it was such a shame we weren't in the motel and then came the staggering realisation we had to report to the ship at 06:30 and navigate the streets of Long Beach absolutely legless. Just four and a half hours away and get the car back, which we had only hired until Sunday night. Oh no.

Born in Stockport - Grew up in the Royal Navy

The journey was awful. Dave Eaton fell asleep at the wheel and nearly crashed but it sort of woke him up and he pressed on to Long Beach. Somehow or other in the pitch black and using only road direction signs, we made it to the dockyard and then alongside the ship by about 06:15. Checked back onboard, got below and got changed for a day's work. The great thing was we didn't have hangovers, at least not until lunchtime but then we knocked off and got a beer and a good kip in our bunks.

Dave had to return the car and nicked off the ship after breakfast but as it was half a day overdue, scratched and the back seat was wobbly they refused to return our deposit. Bastards.

When alongside in the states, the ship received numerous requests from our American cousins. Some would simply want to take a sailor home with them. Any sailor, it didn't matter what size. There they would be feasted, entertained and shown off to family and friends, then returned to the ship none the worse, apart from usually being legless. A ritual we called being "Grippoed". We even had a telephone line advertised as "Dial a Sailor" I shit you not.

Some of the requests were for sporting competition and we got them for both football and rugby. It surprised a lot of us just how good the yanks were at rugby even back in the 70's and there was a thriving set of leagues for the egg chasers.

The football squads were called together for a meeting in the dining hall to consider the requests to play games and there were a few. One of them was for Besty's Bar & Restaurant and I raised my hand to say that will be George Best's pub and was told to wind my neck in and received encouragement such as of course it isn't and that old favourite, shut up you knob.

Anyway, as luck would have it, the only day we could play a game, there was only one team we could play and it was Besty's Bar & Restaurant. On the day, the ex-pat Jocks, Paddy's, Taff's and Englanders living in California confirmed that it was indeed George Best's pub. I beamed and made sure all my team knew. Ha ha.

We lost the game as they had some pretty tasty players, some of whom had been with professional clubs around the UK but it was a great humoured day and we went back to the bar for the traditional post-match drinks.

I was absolutely Hank Marvin and asked a lovely lady behind the bar if I could get something to eat and she asked what I was looking for. When I used the northern term for a sandwich, she went into raptures "A BUTTY" she said in a good Manchester accent, she said she hadn't heard that term for years and went to regale how she had worked for George Best at Slack Alice's and Oscars only a few years before in Manchester.

She took me back into the kitchen and made me up a four-deck beef butty with horseradish sauce on them and then chatted as she watched me demolish them before we returned to the bar.

When we got to the bar it was absolutely rammed and some sort of Mexican stand-off was taking place as an American Football Team had all turned up and demanded it was their night in the bar and the football team, complete with accompanying wives and children would all have to get out. The matelots, never the shy or retiring type had blocked the ex-pat retreat and were squaring up to the AF people.

WHOOOOAAAA said the manager of the bar. WHOOOOOOAAA also said the manager of the football team. No fighting or the bar gets shut down. Right, we need a new method of sorting this out and some bright spark (probably one of us) suggested we settle things with a beer drinking contest.

Who is our best drinker? Well, it was The Head (pronounced HEEEED) a bearded skinny jock who always came to watch the matches and supported Celtic. Full on alcoholic, he could drain a pint in a little over a second. He just tipped em up, opened his throat somehow and the lot would shoot down his throat quicker than you could say Jack Robinson.

They produced someone called ButterBall. A big fat lad of about 20 stone and even those of who knew the prowess of The Head thought this might be a struggle. More so when they said it was going to be a pitcher of beer and not a glass. Four-pint pitchers at that. Shit.

Typical yanks who love to spell out the rules. There will be a second who will hold the pitcher, the referee will count down from 5. On the count of one, the second will pass the pitcher to the drinker, who only then will commence consuming beer. They are proper tossers at times, the yanks.

So, the countdown starts and both lads are staring hungrily at the beer, we get to one and there is a flash of hands as the pitchers are offered and grabbed, then tipped up. The Head drains the four pints in seconds whilst ButterBall is still chewing beer with his goggle eyes staring through the glass, when The Head slams down his empty pitcher and goes berserk and starts looking round for the second pitcher and cannot locate it.

We have to calm him down and say it was only one pitcher and the American Football players start filing out of the bar with ButterBall still trying to see off the pitcher of beer.

Once the AF team left, the expats cannot quite take it all in and as The Head is given a beer to cool him down and told to sip it, we are asked what would have happened if we had lost the beer drinking competition. The wide-eyed expats should not have been surprised to know that we expected the bar to be closed down after winning the fight.

We had some great runs ashore in Long Beach and had a whale of a time and I do remember one doorman in an LA club commenting how amazing that all these guys were born in 1956.... but all good things come to an end and we put back to sea for more exercises with our US Navy friends.

At some point one of the condenser motors blew. This affected the limited air conditioning that we enjoyed down below. In the ensuing attempts to repair by using other motors, our wonderful ships mechanics managed to kill the unit that turned salt water into potable drinking water and one of the stabilisers that kept the ship balanced at sea. Outstanding.

During one of the big exercises with the yanks we were on water rationing, which meant the taps were turned on for about 30 minutes in a morning and once again in the evening. With permission from the skipper, Mike Gretton, we all stopped shaving as it took time and used up water.

Born in Stockport - Grew up in the Royal Navy

The 30 minutes was like a relay race to get into a shower, soap up, rinse off and get out so the next guy could have a go.

The laundry packed in because there was insufficient water to wash our clothes. It was therefore, no surprise to read that Dress of the Day was amended to "Pirate Rig" in other words, an order to wear whatever you want. Oh, what fun was had.

Guys turned to dressed in all sorts of stuff. We had cowboys complete with Stetsons, holsters and cap guns, Indians and people in dinner suits. For a few days Hawaiian shirts were the flavour of the moment on the bridge and we had others dressed as punk rockers and skinheads. We had a bunch of dabtoes dressed as pirates, as they seemed to take the instruction literally and they made themselves wooden swords and had a variety of battles (in their own time) for a laugh.

We still had to work though and in one bit of close manoeuvring with a yank warship, we had a voice message come through to the bridge about what a fine-looking ship the Ambuscade was but what the hell were those things clambering around all over it. Meaning the crew.

Arriving in San Diego, we got all the motors replaced but on departure a big piece of lagging blew out of the funnel, requiring us to remain alongside for weeks waiting for the right bit of Rolls Royce to find the right bit of engine, bring it out and replace it.

San Diego, of course, was where our softball competition winning US Marine's were from and so we made contact again. They hosted us for numerous barbecue's and parties for almost the entire time we were there. We had to tell them our stories and they took some of us out for the day with their families. They were amazing hosts and good people. The instructors from the US Marine Corps Recruitment Depot.

We had full use of the US Navy recreational spaces and played football out on some lovely grass pitches. Our ships rugby team continued to play US teams at a surprisingly good level and enjoyed a number of good social events.

One evening, we had a ship 5 a-side football tournament in a big gym. Whilst trying hard to shoot, I followed through into a block tackle and had to pull up with amazing pain in my big toe. I was substituted and limped off to the side where one of my messmates rendered first aid.

The blood tipping out of my trainer should have indicated the severity of the injury but the lad who looked, calmly said that I had just split the skin and eased my trainer back on. A jeep was radioed in to collect me and take me back to the ship.

Once I was out of sight, the lad with the radio then told the ship that I had a compound fracture of my big toe, which was poking out through a hole in my sock and it was bleeding heavily.

Back on board, I was offered a tablet of some description, which clearly calmed me down. I was pretty chilled then as my sock was cut off and I could see the extent of the injury. I was still quite chilled until the point the Vet tried to stitch the wound as a temporary measure until I could get ashore to the US Navy medical centre. At that point I gave him some shit. Even I knew the bone had to be set first but he didn't seem to have a clue.

So, he shoved a shell dressing over it and wound it tight with bandages and told me to go get my head down and he would sort out transport for in the morning. Which he did.

A jeep came for me and I limped down the gangway and was whisked over the US Navy medical centre. An orderly got some scissors and was shaking his head as he was swearing as he cut away the blood-soaked bandage. He asked me who the fuck had dressed the wound, so I told him. It was the Vet. He roared out laughing saying to all and sundry that the English ship had a Vet onboard. No matter how much I tried to explain the dictionary thing, it was lost in the moment and endured the mirth with the rest of them.

The yank doctor did a good job of setting the bone and stitching me up, gave me a penicillin jab and sent me back to the ship and under the care of the Vet. Haha. It took weeks to heal and is probably why I didn't play football for the ship again. It was still aching when I got home for an extended chrimbo leave at the end of 1978.

We had time for fantastic visits to San Francisco, Vancouver and the logging town of Nanaimo where I reached the age of 21 and celebrated with an outrageous drinking session.

Before that though, I got away with steal of the century. We had a stoker billeted in our mess. A bit of knob, sadly from Stockport, who used to try and start fights with Chinese dhoby guy, who also shared our mess.

The stoker was forever oversleeping. On this particular morning, I was detailed to clean up the mess for the day. A full sweep out, empty the bins, wipe down the table and other flat surfaces. More of a spruce up. But sorted quickly. The door suddenly zoomed open and in walked a bloke in overalls. Probably to wake up the stupid stoker but he didn't knock on the door. A very basic sign of respect in the navy. No-one walked into another mess without knocking and waiting to be invited in. So, I shoved him in the chest pushed him out of the door and slid it shut and shouted "Knock on the door!"

The idiot in the overalls did no more than rush back in, with his arms flailing. So, I punched him straight in the face and knocked him back out into the passageway on his arse and slid the door shut and shouted "Knock on the door you ignorant cunt!"

I am not sure at what moment I realised that he was a Chief Petty Officer, Artificer. It could have been when he slid the door open again to announce he was a Chief Tiffy, or I remembered his name but I slid the door shut in his face again demanding that he knock on the door.

He just stood on the other side of the door making some threatening noises from outside in the passageway and stormed off. I wondered what would happen next...

Shortly afterwards was a familiar pipe. Well familiar to me anyway. "RO1 Perkins, Master At Arms office"...... so I made my way down there.

The Joss was shaking his head slowly when I knocked on his door and he called me in. The Chief Tiffy, sporting a red face was sat in the opposite corner of the office. The Joss told me that the Chief Tiffy was reporting an assault, an extremely serious charge and asked me to explain what had just happened. So, I did.

Born in Stockport - Grew up in the Royal Navy

The Joss turned to the Tiffy and asked a rhetorical question "Did you not knock on the door?" and the Tiffy shook his head. "Off you go Perkins, I will sort this out" and that was that.

I can only assume that there was something going on between the Chief Tiffy and the Joss because there was no more trouble. Well except for two of the big gunners who accosted me in the dining hall demanding to know if I had knuckled their Chief Tiffy. So, I said yes and explained the circumstances. Once they knew he hadn't knocked on the door, they calmed down and said he was a wanker anyway. Haha. I saw him loads of times on the rest of that trip and he kept a wide berth from me.

Anyway, one of our chef's had a cousin working at one of the night clubs in Nanaimo and he arranged for VIP access for the Picnic Club whilst we were there. So as the clock struck midnight on 21st September, my party started. Someone produced bubbly and I began drinking.

The club chucked us out at about 4am I think and I managed to get back onboard and my head down until being rudely awakened by Call the Hands at an unearthly 05:45 for a turn to at 06:30. I stumbled around whatever part of ship I was supposed to be cleaning, painting or polishing and there was a pipe at around 09:00 for RO1 Perkins to report to 2D Mess. I thought shit, what haven't I done and tried to remember if I had made my pit and secured my locker.

I made it down to 2D Mess, which had a sliding door and when I opened it, the mess was in pitch black darkness. I tried to find the light switch when it came on and a packed mess sang "Happy Birthday" whilst shoving a pint of gin and some tonic, into my hand. With shouts of "drink, drink, drink" I did. Though my best was only about half of it and had to give up.

The remaining half was then quickly passed round those present, who all had a gulpers and I was left with a small pyramid of cans of beer to work through. Most people disappeared but someone was drinking with me and I think the guys took turns to make sure I wasn't drinking alone on my birthday and we discussed plans for that evening's extravaganza at the night club.

I am not sure what time I passed out and was completely unaware of anyone trying to wake me for the football match that afternoon or get up for my birthday run ashore. I do know that I woke up kneeling next to my bottom pit, with my torso, head and arms at a crazy angle over the sleeping bag and feeling like shit.

Managing to get vertical in time for evening rounds and then staggering down to the showers, I was able to make myself ship-shape and ready for shore. I got out to the nightclub about 9pm I think and was met by a loud roar from the VIP area and off we went again. Someone did mention that I was in the shit for failing to make the football match but I couldn't care less at that moment.

I did care, when the team manager, our Radio Supervisor, Alfie Marks announced the following day that I was getting a 3-match ban for missing the game but I was expected to support the team and help him with the bags etc. When the ban was over, I had to start back in the second team and don't think I actually got a game with the first team at all after that.

My request to re-take my killicks exam, formally known as the Leading Radio (General) Qualifying Examination went through without a hitch and certainly without any mention of monkey's being made. I passed it with flying colours, so my SCO made me up to acting Leading Radio Operator (General) and I sewed on my hook.

We had a fantastic few day's in Acapulco before heading back through the Panama Canal and I nearly lost my hook a few weeks later when we stopped in Trinidad and Tobago, berthed in the Port of Spain for a Short Maintenance Period and I lost my wallet in a fight with the doormen in the Miramar Club. A fight I didn't start and was just protecting myself and defending my mates.

The Miramar Club was a dodgy old place at the best of time's but we had been attracted in by its cheap cabaret night and the promise of some entertainment. The mesh grill over the bar with one little square to hand your money over and another to receive your drinks, should have been shouting warning signals to us but we were pissed by the time we got there and the five us knew we could handle ourselves anyway.

We were the only white faces in the entire club and so conspicuous, more so when we took up a table right in the middle of the club by the stage. The central stage was used by a trick cyclist, a juggler and fire breather. It was only Clint, a miniature boxer with an innate skill of winding people up like a Jack Russell terrier, that spotted it was the same guy doing all three things. He was just wearing different outfits for each act.

When he came out for the finale, balancing on the unicycle, juggling sticks on fire Clint had noticed he was using a couple of candles on the stage to relight his fire sticks, one of which he cut down with a sword, which he was also juggling. When there was only one candle left, just next to our table, Clint stood up and blew it out.

We collapsed in fits of laughter as the rest of the club sat or stood in silence. Then the posse of doormen rushed in, picked up Clint and threw him down a flight of stairs. We therefore had no choice but to help our mate and fight. So, we did.

I do remember bouncing down the stairs fighting a rear-guard action until the prone and badly winded Clint could be picked up and then we all jumped into a taxi to get back onboard. Where, to my horror, I found I had no wallet and no money but more importantly, no ID card and you cannot get back onboard without one.

I faced the charge of loss of ID card but carefully omitted any details of the fight, as it was superfluous to the occasion and would have only complicated things. It was much simpler to deal with it at The Table, with a "Sorry Sir, it must have fallen out of my pocket" and gone was the evidence of tampering with it to increase my age to 21, bonus. I was now 21 anyway. I didn't lose my hook thankfully, just got a fine of £25 and no pun, which I thought   was a great result considering everything that happened.

The rest of the trip consisted of more exercises with the yanks and our own task force, then we split up and headed off to our home ports. We had to anchor off Guzz overnight and had a "Channel Night" which was minimal staffing at anchor and a few beers. I also had to pack as I was leaving the ship the following day.

Being my last night on the Ambuscade, it was my leaving do and the Picnic Club did me proud with lots of beer and more cakes that should have gone to the wardroom. No loss to them, they had plenty of other stuff to be going on with and as usual, never missed what they didn't have.

Born in Stockport - Grew up in the Royal Navy

At one point in the festivities, Mark Tate, yes the real RO Tate, asked me to help him get SCOT back in synch. And as pissed as I was, I could do it. I couldn't however type, as I could not control my fingers on the keyboard, so I drafted a message to the satcom operating base via Mark, whilst I wanked the levers and got the needle in the green to reset SCOT. Then I bumbled back down below for more beer, without ever noticing the figure lurking in the shadows in the CCR area outside the MCO.

After pulling alongside in Guzz and I had been offered (and accepted) a lift home by Alfie Marks for the cost of two hundred fags on his way up to Glasgow. I was leaving the ship, so had all my kit. Full sailors kit bag, suitcase, holdall and all my rabbits (presents for the family). A Davy Crocket hat and a musket for our Ged and some Mexican jewellery for my Mum, plus some wine for Dad and other odds and sods.

I couldn't leave though without the SCO pulling me to one side and giving me a whispered bollocking about being pissed in the MCO. If it wasn't for my skill in resynchronising the satellite communication system, he said he would have trooped me. But he didn't, he just wished me bon voyage and told me to watch my step. I then hooked up with Alfie on the jetty and told him what's what, which made him laugh. Alfie dropped me off in Stockport as agreed, we shook hands, he took the fags and I was welcomed in by the family.

Dad had sold his council house and bought a 3-bedroom property with a massive garden, on Hillbrook Road in Offerton. Strange to leave home in the spring and arrive at a new home at Christmas, one that I never felt at home at, for that very reason probably. It wasn't my house.

Furthermore, all my treasures disappeared. Odd things that meant something to me as a kid. Also lost without trace was my porn collection, found by our Ged when they tipped the wardrobe out... for fuck sake. Someone somewhere must have got a cheap thrill for free when he chucked them out.

David asked me if I wanted to go out on a four-some as a blind date with one of his colleagues from work, probably encouraged by Mum, so we went downtown to spend some of my chrimbo wad on some new clothes. David had a good eye for fashion and helped me out with some good advice. I bought my first decent jacket and pants, a load of shirts and some jumpers.

We went out in Dads car. David driving as I didn't have a licence. He picked up a girl he used to go to school with and then we drove into the town centre to pick up this lovely young lady. Her name was Bev and she worked with David at Curtess shoes.

Bev wasn't sure about the blind date when David invited her, as she remembered the mouthy matelot brother from earlier in the year but knew he had two brothers and assumed I would be the other one.

When she got into the car, Bev thought "oh no, it's the wanker" whilst I hardly remembered her and thought she looked gorgeous.

From that inauspicious start, we did enjoy a nice meal and a reasonably entertaining evening in a hotel restaurant up in the hills. I asked Cupid (our David) if I could see her again. Bev came to our family Christmas party with her Dad, as a guest of David and I managed to arrange a second date when we were supposed to watch a movie.

The movie that was showing was not the one we thought it would be and my salvage move was to take her for a drink in a cosy little pub near the Town Hall and I proper charmed her socks off .

We dated like mad all over Christmas and into the New Year. I was infatuated with her. I had a total of about five weeks leave and had to report back to HMS Antrim on Monday 22nd January 1979 before transferring on to my Leading Hands Professional Qualifying Course at HMS Mercury on 24th January, just a couple of days later.

I planned to propose to Beverly after our whirlwind romance on the Sunday before I had to depart in a moment I had hoped would be romantic. I had a spot picked out in Vernon Park, just a short walk from our house.

Bev had been invited for Sunday dinner, following which I would have to get the train south to report to the ship in the morning.

I announced to all and sundry that Bev and I would take a stroll in the park. Mum said "Great idea, you can take the dog for a walk" which I thought was okay cover for my private mission "and our Ged as well, he could do with some exercise".

"MacTavish" the plucky and noisy West Highland White Terrier had its tail up and a lead in his mouth, Ged jumped out of his chair to grab his football, so I grabbed Bev and off we went.

Plan B was formulated on the walk through Woodbank Park, playing passing with Ged and holding Bev's hand whilst the dog was on a lead pulled by Bev.

Our Ged, like most kids, was a sucker for a bit of a challenge and almost any form of competition. You should ask him about wringing the last drops out of a wet flannel sometime for a full explanation but suffice to say, on his bath night, no matter how hard he tried, he would hand over what he presumed to be a "dry flannel" and I would wring a few more drops out and he had to take the punishment of a cup of cold water over his head. Ha, ha, never got old that one. Who knows, one day my children may experience the same challenge...

So, we got to the spot I had chosen, a little bridge in a wooded and secluded part of the park. No-one was about, other than my gooseberry little brother. I shouted to Ged that I bet he couldn't run to the ice age rock in the park a few hundred yards from the bridge and back in less than 60 seconds.

Without any further ado, he shot off and I was choosing the moment in our conversation when I could drop down on one knee and propose. That moment came but before I could go down on one knee Ged reappeared and shouted as to which ice age stone he should run to?

I shouted back that it was the smooth one that you can slide down. He nodded and ran off furiously to break whatever world record had been set and the moment passed.

I couldn't take the risk of his imminent return so told Beverly that I had planned to go down on one knee and propose but just blurted out, would you marry me. She said yes and we kissed. Then the red-faced Ged re-appeared demanding to know what his time was. Brilliant.

We went home and told Mum and Dad that we would be getting engaged.

A little over a year later, we got married on 3rd May 1980, at St. Albans Church, in Offerton just round the corner from Hillbrook Road but we will get to that in due course.

In the month of May 2020, we celebrated our Ruby Wedding Anniversary, just the two of us as we were in lockdown during the COVID-19 Pandemic and separated from our family that was yet to be created...

I managed to get a bouquet of 40 red roses delivered and we organised a take-away from one of our favourite restaurants, Turquoise in Cheadle. We also exchanged new wedding bands. What a pair of old romantics.

Chapter Three

HMS Mercury

Born in Stockport - Grew up in the Royal Navy

I started on my LRO(G) Professional Qualifying Course back at radio school and my hook got me a single cabin in one of the accommodation blocks.

One or two of my new classmates were familiar from my travels, Keith Stansfield from my time at Northwood and Jamie Stewart off the Antrim. A good group of lads who liked a beer and a game of football.

The course was tough but eminently doable from my perspective and I did well. We had a pretty sociable routine on the course, in the classrooms all day, five a-side football in the gym, whatever duty we were rostered for, usually patrolling and/or beers in the Mercury NAAFI club.

I would get home as often as I was able to and a lot of my money went on train fares and cadging lifts in cars as far north as I could, then purchasing train tickets from wherever I could get dropped off to spend time with Bev.

We used to go to the County Club, a little nightclub owned by one of the lesser gangsters in town and a director of Stockport County, Josh Lewis. Allegedly part of the famous Quality Street Gang. Josh was an amiable club owner and I never saw any trouble there. It was the 1970's and cabaret shows were all the rage. We would be entertained by good comedians, decent bands and the occasional magician but thankfully no fire eating, juggling, unicyclists....

I would walk over from Offerton to Cheadle Heath, where Bev lived with her Mum and stepdad, then walk her onto Castle Street in Edgeley for a couple of drinks in one of the pubs, then across to the County Club for the show and a dance later. When the club closed, I would walk Bev back home for a kiss and cuddle, then I would walk home to Offerton. A two- or three-mile walk. We only used taxi's if it was raining.

On my way back home from dropping Bev off in Cheadle Heath one night, I was yomping down Castle Street in Edgeley in fine fettle and enjoying the fresh air at about 2am when two lads peeled away from the shadows of the KwikSave Supermarket, one in front and one behind me. The one in the front said hand over your wallet and there won't be any trouble and I said something like too late as I butted him and followed it up with a punch on his way down.

I turned to face the lad behind me but he was off on a runner already. Despite a belly full of beer, I was a very fit 21-year-old and ran after him. I caught up with him in seconds and tripped him up. He went sprawling and was crying and screaming before I hit him. Only once or twice. Then I jogged back for the first one but he had gone by then. Fucking hyenas picked the wrong one tonight. I walked home full of myself.

The killicks course at Mercury was in full flow and as I said, the content was tough but I was getting through it all. Some of my mates though fell by the wayside and our class was a tad smaller by the time we got to the point of weekly exams. You could have one failure, resit it and pass. Any further failings and it was straight out of the door and off back to your ship. One strike and you're out sort of thing.

We played a lot of football. Several 11 a-side games on the crappy pitches at the back of the camp and oodles of 5 a-side in the recreation centre. Which was to provide the venue for my second encounter with a ghost. However, we will start with the first one.

The IRA threat to the whole country and for the military in particular was a constant challenge. HMS Mercury was an "open" camp with a local road running through it dividing the accommodation blocks and the main establishment and required constant patrolling when the threat was high. Patrols were lessened in the daytime as there were so many servicemen on training courses creating a constant presence. In the evening and throughout the night, there were many.

I was part of a 16-man team on nights, patrolling in pairs. Standard Operating Procedure (SOP) was two hours on watch, 2 hours off watch, with 4 x pairs on patrol at any one time and back up in the gatehouse. We were issued with the old faithful wooden truncheons with lead weights on the end. Pretty lethal in a hand-to-hand fight but fucking useless if the IRA turned up with AK-47's or Armalite rifles... bright white webbing contrasted well with the No.8 navy blue pants and big great coats. You could see us coming for miles. May be that was the idea.

On the 02:00 – 04:00 stint, it was snowing quite heavily and so the lad I was paired with on duty, slid into the squash courts to stay dry and keep warm as the radiators were on 24/7 in the entrance hall. The plan was one sits on the floor with his back to the radiator and the other stand guard at the doorway.

I woke up with the lad from the doorway asleep next to me leaning onto the radiator. Fuck. So, I woke him up and dragged him out to show some willing and told him to be careful with the door, as it was on a pretty wicked return spring. He wasn't awake as he stumbled out and the door crashed shut. It had stopped snowing and the air was very still and had been utterly quiet as the boom of the door closing echoed around us. Then I saw him. About 50 yards away in front of the old hall where the wardroom was.

A bloke in dark clothing, big greatcoat on and a dark hat. No white webbing. Probably an officer out checking stuff. Shit, we had to challenge him with the standard "Halt, who goes there?" he turned to face us but didn't reply. So, I shouted the challenge again and he just shrugged and walked away from us. Shit. We had to follow him but he went over the lawn in front of the big hall and walked straight into the woods.

We got to the lawn and the other lad asked where he had gone and I told him into the woods. Right, we need to follow his footsteps. The virgin snow showed the footprints of the two of us but no other. We looked all over the lawn and towards the woods but couldn't see any other prints..... at which point we got on the radio and called it in. All the others were already back in the guardhouse handing over, so we hot footed it back to share our story.

The second experience was far more involved. I was on a set of evening patrols, my last one was 22:00 – 23:59. We got a call over the radio to proceed to sickbay and investigate a report. We got to sickbay and the duty nurse, under their own SOP would not open the door but spoke to us through a window and said someone had been locked in the Recreation Centre, look. She pointed to a figure stood in the shadows of the pool area. Right, better get the Rec Centre keys and let him out. Odd that he hadn't used one of the wall phones to call the gatehouse.

We tracked to the gatehouse and back with the keys, opened up and went inside. The pair of us shouted out and turned on all the lights but no-one appeared. We did as good a search as two people can, commencing with the pool area, which felt colder than the outside. Probably something to do with water condensing or something. We checked the changing rooms, main hall. All the offices and weight room were locked up anyway but we still opened them and checked. Satisfied that no-one was there, we were discussing it as we took the keys back to the gatehouse when we got a call to return to the sick bay.

The nurse didn't open the window this time, she just pointed across the way to the pool and there was the guy again. This time I radioed into the gatehouse who pulled two other patrols in whilst we stayed to reassure the nurse and keep an eye on where the guy went.

The other two patrols got the keys, opened the Rec Centre and carried out a systematic search. As the lights came on in the Rec Centre, the figure at the window turned away from us and just disappeared. I remember looking at my companion who stood open-mouthed and the nurse, who swiftly closed the curtain and we made our way over to carry out an external patrol of the Rec Centre and checked all the doors, which were locked.

There is no rational explanation for either of these two events. I have seen other apparitions throughout my life and I have become less concerned about them as I have got older. I know what I have seen. They don't scare me anymore. Not much does to be honest.

Whilst I was at Mercury, I used the opportunity to get down to Pompey and catch up with my old Antrim mates who were all RA by then. I stayed at Frank's love nest with Amy and with Gabby, who was now sharing a flat with Brummie Lowe in Southsea. I collected my photo scrap albums and what was left of my record collection.

We had a good few piss-ups in Southsea. Gabby's landlady Mrs B. used to fire up her upright cleaner very early on Saturday mornings to hoover the hallways and landings. I am sure she banged it into the skirting boards on purpose as it was a pretty rude awakening.

On a freezing cold morning I lay in a sleeping bag on a mattress on the floor. Scouse Chadwick was dossed down on the settee. Brummie Lowe was in a single bed on one side of the room and Gabby was sharing his double bed with a wren writer called Sue.

My bladder was screaming at me to get to the loo, which was probably the reason I woke up. It was ahead of the usual Mrs B. hoover assault, so the place was silent. I heard the wren whisper to Gabby "Get it up" and his whispered reply was "I can't" meaning, he didn't think it was right with a room full of his mates but we didn't see it that way...

I sat up and said, "You can't get it up?" followed almost in chorus by Scouse and Brummie also saying something similar and we all burst out laughing as Hayes did his best to explain then told us all to fuck off as he and Sue set about themselves. Brilliant.

I passed my course with flying colours and my reward was to have my Leading Hand's rate confirmed once I had completed the two-week Leadership Course at HMS Raleigh.

Chapter Four

HMS Raleigh

There were two of us off our radio course, an alcoholic who was based on HMS Walrus, one of the navy tugs used to pull subs about up in Faslane, Barry Whittaker, a grizzled lad from Stafford and me.

At lunchtime at Mercury, the bar opened for 45 minutes. No opportunity to get pissed but enough time for Barry to sup three barley wines. The bar only sold bottles or draft beer. No glasses of wine and no spirits. The three barley wines at 10% were a good injection of alcohol and would see him through the day until the bar opened for the evening.

Barry got back early from a weekend home on time, on a Saturday afternoon. It was unheard of. One of the NAAFI girls was from Stafford and had hitched a lift home with Barry. She offered him some petrol money but he said no he was going to Stafford anyway. She invited him into her parent's pub for a quick thank you beer instead so he did and had no further recollections of the rest of the day.

Barry woke up in his own bed, with his mother poking him with a broom. Barry's first thought was that he didn't remember taking a bar of chocolate to bed with him…. Evidently, he had followed through in bed and it was everywhere. He had previous form and they threw him out. So, when he returned to Mercury, it was with all his worldly goods. Which didn't turn out to be that much to be honest.

We agreed to convert our two travel warrants into petrol chits for his car, which he promptly exchanged at the first service station for fuel and cash. More than enough for two nights B&B and a load of beer chits. We stayed at Aggie Weston's for two nights and then checked into Drake on the Sunday. The lad could certainly drink.

Over many beers, Barry explained, that he had it on good authority that we would be required to complete the basic RN fitness test first thing on Monday morning and that we should hold something back, then over the two-week course, we can easily demonstrate improvements.

After registering on Sunday, we were instructed to turn to early on Monday morning, in PT gear for the RN Fitness Test. Just as Barry had predicted. The PTI leading the course then announced that lots of people are under the false impression you should hold something back on the first day, so that your result can be improved upon. The course is all about throwing in your total effort and demonstrating commitment. He expected us to do just that.

The test was a simple affair. Run a mile in under ten minutes. Sprint 300 yards in under a minute. Do a standing jump to a distance greater than your height and a whole series of sit-ups, press-ups and burpees to a minimum number and within a set time limit.

Full of beer from the weekend, I threw up at the end of winning the 300-yard sprint and the PTI held me up by the neck of my t-shirt and announced that this was the sort of effort needed to push yourself to the limit. I thought it was just the beer. Hey ho.

At the end of the tests and well before morning break, three lads were sent back to their ships as having failed their fitness test, which would be a threat to their acting rate if they could not get a place back on the Leadership Course and pass it, within twelve months. The three departed in some shame and one of them was Barry.

The two weeks were all about effort. It was almost like being back in basic training again when we first joined up. We double marched everywhere. Several times, we double marched for about ten miles at a time, just chuntering along like a human train. The steady rhythmic beating of boots on tarmac took us a long way. I loved it. I still think of it when I am chubby shuffling (slow jogging) these days, as it's about the same pace. Twelve minutes a mile.

Every morning commenced with two hours of PT, followed by a five-mile run. My body was getting used to rejecting the previous night's ale, with dry retching and I can remember a PTI jogging on the spot next to me (they just cannot keep still) as I knelt in the road outside of the camp throwing up. "No breakfast?" he queried as I managed a perfunctory nod in reply "I suggest you make breakfast and have some sausages at least". It seemed good advice.

So next morning, I managed to make breakfast and had sausage, eggs and beans. No toast. As we neared the five-mile marker point, the base gatehouse, I felt the familiar feeling and threw up in a ditch. The same PTI (still jogging on the spot) laughed and said, "I see you had the sausage and beans then" and carried on running through the gate, whilst I gathered myself and was overtaken by most of the class.

I solved the problem by drinking slightly less, eating a lot less but never-the-less, eating something. I also held back a lot on the two hours of PT, getting told off for not doing enough press-ups, sit-ups and burpees. Therefore, conserving some energy for the run. I finished third. So that became my routine and I held top five finishes on the morning run every day for the remainder of the course.

Large elements of the Leadership Course were just that, different methods of being able to demonstrate leadership. Presenting to the class, understanding basic man-management approaches, culminating in the Practical Leadership Tests (PLT's). A series of almost real-life exercises designed to push a young leader to his limits in achieving the tasks set. Followed up by a number of one-to-one discussions on our individual performance, reviews and reflection by the cadre of instructors.

I had never presented anything in my life. Never considered as a skill at school I imagine, therefore I was a novice. The first time we were asked to present for seven minutes, it was on a subject card given to us the day before. Mine was Wales. I decided to deliver it with some humour, as was and still is, my style.

On the day, the guy before me had stood up with one sheet of small notebook paper, the serrated edge still looking rough where he had ripped it out of a book. He looked very nervous and so unprepared, as he stood up and the paper was shaking in his hands. He continually looked at it and up at us, then down again. He said his talk was about Campanology.

I turned to the lad next to me and said, that's the art of bellringing, which was immediately confirmed by our nervous speaker who stammered that it was the art of bellringing. Long pause. He said, there are three types of bell. Long pause. Big bells, more shaking of his hands and the up and down movement of his head has not stopped, middle sized bells, as the class start to shake and hold in fits of giggling, when someone shouted out "and little bells!" to which he nodded enthusiastically yes, little bells and we all burst out laughing.

The class instructor stood up and gave us all a right bollocking. This was a serious matter, nothing to laugh about at all. Do you understand that? I guess the complete silence satisfied him as he indicated for me to take his place and deliver my presentation. Which started out something like, I am going to talk about Wales, not the big black things that float around the sea heading harpoons and slapped my OHP slide with a cartoon of a whale wearing a red and white scarf with an arrow stuck in its head but the little country to the left of England. I had planned a pause for the laughter which did not come….

I completed it, inside the time limit but too much inside the time limit, as I had allowed for some response to my funny-ish slides and discussion about singing, rugby and caravan parks.

My next presentation had to be about a subject of our own choice and for fifteen minutes. I chose the Halifax Building Society and government scheme to help first time buyers, by matching what you saved. For every £1 you put into your account, the scheme matched it with a £1 up to a limit of about £500. I used it because it was something I had explored with Bev and we had a joint account there. We both saved about £50 a month each and the Halifax / Government, matched it. It was going to be a deposit on our first house.

During the presentation, we had agreed to give each other hand signals on strategic timed points of five- minute intervals, with a countdown at one-minute intervals on the last five, thus ensuring I finished in good time.

I had got the nod for the last five and was on the fourth of my last five minutes, when I wrapped up the presentation without giving the vital contact details but said I am sure you can find out if you go into your local building society. The instructor waved me to go on as he was completely entranced with the free money thing as he and his wife were planning to buy their own house and move out of married quarters. So, I did.

I got top marks for my presentation and handed over a lot of material to the grateful instructor.

We had an orienteering exercise over Dartmoor where we had to collect a series of codes from hilltop marker posts. The class was split into three smaller teams of about ten. Ours had some good runners in it, so I proposed an idea and led the team. It was a two-day event, 24 miles on the Saturday and 14 miles on the Sunday.

My suggestion was to send a runner up to each marker point, whilst the rest of the class carried all the tents, victuals and other kit as a caravan moving along the route from the start to the finish line. The runners, not carrying any kit, then darted off at the tangents to collect the data. A winning idea I thought, as our team finished the task early.

However, the instructors, watching us from hilltops and driving round the area in land rovers, witnessed everything and dismissed all the points we gathered meaning we finished last. Despite gathering all the codes and smashing the course time, all our team points and my leadership points were dismissed for breaking the team up and incurring risk. My defence that there was nothing in the rules that said we couldn't, didn't cut the mustard.

Days later, we headed to a cove that the Navy used for a variety of training exercises, called Pier Cellars. Still smarting from winning and then losing all my points for our orienteering exercise on Dartmoor, I went at the day with some gusto.

I had already ripped holes in my hand sliding down ropes on the sand cliffs to win the team relay race around the obstacle course and flushed with that success, I failed miserably to use the block and tackle correctly in my task of getting my team down to the jetty off the cliff.

So, the first 9 guys are safely lowered but the last guy has to death slide down. We had agreed together what we did, with the lightest guy going last, so we knew what we had let ourselves in for.

The instructor said later in the debrief that one of the PTI's didn't actually see the kid slide into the waiting clutch of nine with our arms held wide and knock us all over like skittles, because he could see what was about to happen and collapsed in hysterics....

They deducted all my leadership points for that one as well....

We had to go out to other places to complete some of the PLT's, one of them was an old fort. We had to get things like a one-ton block of stone pulled up and over the ramparts. Pick up an injured person from a pit and haul him out in a rigid stretcher and stuff like that. We motored out to the "dead fleet" a load of old ships anchored out in the sound, and carried out damage control exercises, fight fires and capture a deranged drunken sailor armed with a fire axe. Honestly.

The deranged matelot, played superbly by one of the Leading Aircrewmen, was swinging a five-foot fire axe madly around his head and shouting. We subdued him after shooting a high- pressure fire hose at him for a couple of minutes, so that he dropped the axe and was shot into a corner of the compartment, then we dived on him using some smelly mattresses as protection. He screamed that he was wet through, bruised and had dropped the fucking axe but it was an opportunity to scuffle, so we did until we were ordered off him by a laughing instructor. Great fun.

At the end of the course, we had our final results and my assessment will sound very familiar to anyone who knows me.

"An intelligent and confident Leading Hand who thinks quickly and is not afraid to take the initiative.

He needs to blend his innate need to humour everyone by realising not every situation requires a laugh.

Impetuous and sometimes downright reckless, he needs to consider the health and safety of all of his comrades in a smarter way.

He is a natural leader and is often consulted by others in leadership positions because he thinks differently and can see innovative solutions. Some of which work.

Excellent level of fitness and not afraid to throw himself into the fray.

Passed."

And so, I had, which meant I was now a full Leading Hand confirmed. Leading Radio Operator (General). A good achievement and one of the navy's youngest LRO's.

The course had ended and we could go home for the weekend before moving back to our ships or onto whichever draft our friends or was that fiends, at HMS Centurion the administrative centre of the Royal Navy had sent us. In my case, it was back to Northwood for a short duration.

One of the boys, Smudge Smythe, a Leading Aircrewman from Halifax offered me a lift north in his Triumph Spitfire, if we shared the travel warrants as petrol chits and cash. Which I did.

On the M5 somewhere south of Taunton, his engine blew up. Sort of. A piston rod snapped and burst his engine casing, causing a small fire, which failed to respond to a can of coke and a bottle of lemonade being poured over it by Smudge and me when we got out on the hard shoulder. We did drag out all our kits bags, holdalls etc. to be safe as we both expected the car to burst into flames.

Thankfully, a lorry pulled over and the driver had a small fire extinguisher, which he used to good effect before driving off with our grateful thanks.

I asked Smudge if he was in the RAC or AA? To which he replied, neither. Smudge trekked to the nearest emergency road-side telephone and called for help.

A tow truck appeared after a short while, hooked up the Spit and dragged us off the motorway to a yard in the middle of nowhere. His fee to take the car, Smudge and me to Halifax was 33p a mile. Each way. A grand total of £148.50 if I recall.

Smudge wasn't having any of it and used a call box to speak to his Dad, who was in the pub. So, he called several of his mates, who were all in the pub. So, he rang the pub and found out that no-one was fit to drive, even if they could contemplate a long-haul to Taunton and back. Smudge, therefore, reluctantly agreed to the haul and we set off after the Spit was fitted firmly onto a trailer.

Plan A had been for Smudge to drive me home, on his way to Halifax. Now we moved to Plan B. I would get dropped off at Knutsford Services, where my Dad would pick me up. However, we had to move to Plan C, due to the slow speed of the driver. He incessantly stopped at service stations to call his base to find out if he had a return casualty to make his journey even more rewarding. This meant we would not pass Knutsford until well after midnight. My Dad was on an early bus shift on the Saturday morning and so needed his kip.

Plan C was to continue to Halifax and sort out transport in the morning.

Smudge didn't need to wake up his parents, they were already waiting up for us. A good old Irish family, Mrs Smythe had a fry up on the go and a pot of tea waiting for us. Will the driver be joining us? The driver smiled expectantly and nodded. No said Smudge, who was fed up with him by then and not happy he had to write out three cheques as the driver noted his cheque withdrawal limit on his card was £50.

So, we had the fry up and went to bed and he fucked off south back to Somerset.

Got up fairly early-ish I suppose on the Saturday morning, to the smell of another fry up as Mrs Smythe continued to demonstrate all those good-natured things we expect from the Irish, big hugs and lots of cooked food. Smudges Dad then stated he would drive me home to Stockport, despite my protestations that a lift to the railway station would be enough, I am big enough to get home from there but he pointed to my massive kit bag and assorted hand luggage arguing that I would struggle and so I reluctantly agreed to the lift.

They dropped me off at Stockport bus station and would not take any money from me. Smudges Dad turned the car round and I flagged him down to chuck a folded-up fiver in through window as they drove past with Smudge swearing at me and his Dad laughing. A great family. In those quirks of fate, I never crossed paths with Smudge again sadly.

Chapter Five

HMS Warrior

On the 21ˢᵗ of May 1979 I joined HMS Warrior for a second stint and took up a role at the not-so-secret, secret bunker not far from Watford.

It would be hard for me to describe anything I did on this particular draft without touching on its purpose, so I cannot. Suffice to say that it was a Top Secret posting and I had to be Positively Vetted to take up my job there.

However, I did find the source of the MODUK version of the national and world news that each ship received, every day as one quirk of the job was to drive out to a newsagent and pick up a copy of every single available daily newspaper during the night shift and deliver them to a 3-ringer (Commander) in one of the offices.

He would then hand in selected sheets from each paper, with sections of text circled off with a marker as suitable to go out to the men, back into the Communications Centre.

Given the nature of the operation where we worked, I have often thought it a particularly odd job. Maybe they contained hidden messages for others, who knows? What I do know is, one of us would type them up and create the six-pager that was transmitted to every ship, in every corner of the world, every day.

I also know that as a Leading Hand, I was given a quite menial task that in any other place, would have been carried out by rates, far more junior than mine.

The role had a quality element to it. As each signal was transmitted, live feeds from four different aerial sites were presented on four separate teleprinters. Any error, on any part of any signal, on any of the teleprinters, required a manual intervention before the message was complete, with any errors typed in by yours truly.

It was tiring, exacting on your concentration and I missed some of the errors. Maybe it was my insistence not to wear my spectacles, perhaps it was my resistance to delivering such a menial task maybe I was just too fucking tired. It could have been any combination of the lot to be honest.

After my second week, I had got called into the office by the Fleet Chief who ran that particular part of the whole communications centre and told that I was on the bottom of the quality control list with the most errors.

To be fair, I did try hard but it was a thankless task. Each message was repeated a number of times throughout the day and with all the fantastic communications kit the military had, thought it was a waste of time chasing elementary errors that could easily be re-read correctly, for example the letter e missing from the word the, is so easy.

I remained at the bottom of the Fleet Chief's "blacklist" until I departed on the 23rd of November 1979 to pick up a minesweeper in refit in Chatham dockyard.

I did try to get out of the draft by explaining my poor sea legs on smaller vessels. Whilst keeping me fairly trim, often resulted in me carrying a bucket around with some bleach in the bottom of it.

However, as I had never actually reported sick with sea sickness, I would have to go through a period of time and take some medication but the draft stood. So, I headed off to the Dinner Time Session as we nicknamed HMS Soberton, pennant number M1200.

Before that there is still time to talk about opening a bank account, "The Bungalow" and some tension with the security guards at Northwood, usually dressed as Royal Marines.

As my Leading Rate had been confirmed, I was invited into a briefing with others, on the move to monthly payments into a bank account. I didn't have one. I had a Post Office savings account but that didn't carry any weight in these proceedings evidently. It had to be a bank and a current account. Great.

The briefing was delivered by someone from one of the big banks, I think it was Barclays and led by one of the Fleet Chief Writers. The two chaps patiently explained that from a certain date, all monthly payments to each matelot would have to be made into a bank account and no longer would we, as Leading Hands, stand to attention every two weeks with our pay books and receive cash.

The bank man went on to explain that for this service, the bank would charge some fees and worse still, if we drew out more than we had, and I have to say that I did not understand the concept of "drawing out more money than you had" as you either had money, or you didn't. That an unapproved overdraft would incur significant financial penalties.

So, me being me, put my hand up. Then, I started. I work and the navy pays me my wages. Yes, say the two chaps at the front. I continue. But no longer will I get cash but my wages will be paid into a bank account, where I have to pay you to hold my money until I want to spend it, in which case I have to go to the bank to draw it out. Yes, say both chaps nodding. I end with, well its simple then, you are not having my money.

Which is when all the ruckus started. My colleagues present, all got in the same mood as me and agreed that it was stupid to have to pay someone else to hold our money. So, I sat back and watched it all unfold. Lots of shouting, lots of explaining that this was how the navy was going to modernise wage payments. To which I asked if the navy would pick up the cost of banking as it was their idea not mine. Cue pandemonium, which only ended when the Fleet Chief gave us all a verbal bollocking and a direct instruction to shut up and open a bank account.

I didn't comply.

I stood for two more payments, cash in hand, saluting with my pay book held in my outstretched hand, when I was taken to one side and ordered to open a bank account that week. I successfully argued that I would open a bank account at home and not in Watford or anywhere else. That would be okay they responded. But I couldn't afford to go home said I, as I have run out of travel warrants.

So, I got a surprising free travel warrant to get back to Stockport on one of my three days off to open an account, which I did at the robbing bastards I thought Barclays were. However, it was the bank of choice of my father, who remains a loyal customer of theirs to this day. I'm not.

Some of the guys in our watch went RA and took their spending power into the world of privately rented accommodation. They did a deal on a tin roofed shack that was nailed to the back of a betting office in Kings or Bishops Langley, just a few miles from Northwood.

One of the lads, Terry ran a gold Ford Escort Ghia and took the three of them back and forth for their watches. It was also the home of our watch parties, every 8 days for the rest of the time I was there. The rest day on day three of the standard eight-day roster.

As good as they tried to make it, the place was a shithole but a very cheap shithole and it turned them quite a few beer chits in the difference between what the navy paid each of them as a daily allowance and what the three of them paid the landlord in weekly rent.

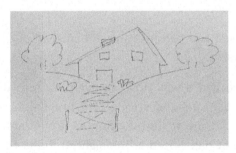

In order to attract a good selection of guests, Terry knowing my cartoon capabilities, asked me to sketch out some party invitations to "The Bungalow" so I decided to make it look as inviting as possible and it did look something like this. Which of course, did not look anything like the breezeblock built shack it was.

Once people got over the initial shock, it turned into a proper party palace and very much part of the social scene. Bring a bottle. Don't cause any trouble and you are in.

I had a couple of run-ins with a wanker of a bootneck security guard. He wasn't the biggest Royal Marine, probably my size and he used to pick fights in the Galaxy Club with pissed matelots. Never anyone sober.

So that's what I did on one of the club nights. I stayed sober and when he did his usual trick of bumping into a pissed matelot and calling him out for spilling his beer, I stepped in and told him and his mates exactly what happened. If he wanted a scrap, then here I was.

We went outside and squared up. Not sure who won the fight but I won the moral ground and I know I put him down a couple of times. It all ended square I guess but I wasn't backing down or walking away.

So on to Terry and the guys first party, one of my bezzy oppo's ever, Paul Finch and I had taken a mixture of white wine and beer. We made ourselves a new cocktail of pints of beer / wine mixers. Quite lethal in the end. Terry asked me to watch the door and not let any idiots in.

A taxi rocked up and a load of bootnecks climbed out, including the one I had the scrap with. I stood there and announced that they could all come in except you, pointing to my previous opponent. They decided to enter and leave the trouble causer to disappear in the taxi. I think they thought he was a wanker too.

The party went well and I am not sure if I crashed out there or we got a taxi back to the base.

Another night, we had a wild drive through Watford with a very pissed Terry avoiding police cars and driving over roundabouts. It was hilarious and he didn't get caught. It started after we broke the barrier in a multi-storey car park that had closed at midnight. It didn't take much to break but someone must have seen us and called the police.

Earlier, we had all been on a watch run ashore to Bailey's the big night club in Watford. I didn't have a jacket so Beryl, one of the Wren RO's said Polly, put this over your shoulder and they can see you have a jacket.

One of the bouncers told me that a jacket was required to enter Baileys and I shrugged and pointed to the jacket over my shoulder. He replied with a dry comment that I had to wear it to get in, not have it over my shoulder. Great.

Now Beryl was a big, bosomed girl but in a less than average sized frame, which meant her jacket was about four sizes too small for me. I looked like a chimp as I managed to get it over my shoulders, which were pulled up tight but the arms of the jacket only just came past my elbows. I looked a right cunt.

It clearly didn't fit but the lovely ladybird brooch on the front and lovely smell of Beryl's perfume made the borrow look so obvious. Everyone around me burst out laughing but the good thing was that the bouncers saw the funny side and let me in.

Once inside, the jacket came off and got handed back to Beryl, who checked it over to see how much I had stretched it…. Cheers.

My time at the fun palace that Northwood was came to an end and I shunted off down to Chatham by train to pick up my last sea draft in the mob. The small and beautifully formed Sobie.

Before that, Bev and I had an engagement party in the small function room above The War Office, real name the Gardeners Arms, just down the road from where we live now. A lovely do. Lots of music and lots of dancing.

The pub was nicknamed The War Office as it was the place that recruits signed on to join the military for both world wars. The landlord at the time of our do was an ex-Royal Marine sergeant. A very good but tough guy called Clarkey. He was there for years.

Born in Stockport - Grew up in the Royal Navy

Chapter Six

HMS Soberton

I joined HMS Soberton, the first royal navy ship to be completely refitted by civilians in a military dockyard on 24th November 1979.

The ship was in bits alongside, with loads of civilian dockyard workers crawling over her. The ship was being managed from the suite of portable buildings alongside on the jetty and that's where I reported to.

The skipper welcomed me on board and handed me over to the Coxswain, Mick O'Gara, an absolute legend. The skipper was Lieutenant Commander Jonathan Band, who later in his career became Rear Admiral Sir Jonathan Band, Commander in Chief, Royal Navy. A great guy and we all knew back then that he was destined for higher things. Known affectionately by us as "JB".

The ships company gradually built up over those first few months I was onboard. Others had been there almost for the duration. We were based in the accommodation blocks in HMS Pembroke the training school for Navy Chefs that very few ever passed successfully, at least that's what the rest of the ships company always ribbed the chefs about. Toughest course in the Navy. No-one ever passes. Haha.

First thing though, I got drafted back to HMS Mercury for a small ships course. Learn the black art of the Buntings so I could do my bit in tactical signalling etc. and slow down my Morse Code for operating the flashing signalling lanterns.

The Soberton had two sparkers, no buntings. My other half was Brigham (Alan) Young, a grizzled lad who had branch changed to RO. We had a lot of fun.

I was on the small ships course at Mercury late in the year. First weekend I was duty, doing the familiar Bikini Black patrols because of the IRA threat, so didn't get home at a time of great strife and pressure. I was also billeted in a mess full of "Deeps or Smellies" our submariner cousins.

They welcomed me late on the first night when they found out they were sharing with a "Skimmer or Target" with a typical initiation ceremony. Four of them turned me over in my bed, in one swift movement. Leaving me nose down on the bed springs with a perfectly made bed above me.

I managed to wriggle out and re-made my bed, whilst they climbed into their pits laughing and joking and partly waiting for my response. However, revenge is often a dish best served cold, so I bided my time for an hour or so until they were all snoring away fast asleep. Probably thinking I was a wimp.

The tactics I decided to employ were based around a rush. I quietly exited my pit and limbered up a bit in the dark. Then I ran at the first bed shouted loudly and just lifted and tipped, no finesse and then rushed onto the second and then a third continuing to roar a challenge. I intended doing as many as I could before the inevitable backlash ending in a fist fight, which I inevitably lost as they all piled onto me.

Fight over, we stood panting in the dark until someone turned on the mess lights. Then there was laughter and some good-natured banter and I knew that standing up for myself, as always, turned up trumps and I was welcomed into their company. Mainly for my display but also that I was on a "boat" not a ship.

Funny thing about the Navy. Minesweepers and Submarines are referred to as boats and all the other stuff as ships. Anyway, evening entertainment was drinking with the submariners and getting up to no good with them. We had a few skirmishes but mainly it was piss-taking and out-drinking anyone who fancied it.

My daily routine was to finish classes, get an early supper and call home. Alternating between Mum & Dad and my girlfriend and intended, Beverly. Then I would shower and get into the club.

Bev and I had discussed lots about the future and had agreed to put off our wedding until after I left the Navy. I had made the decision and in the summer of 1979 had handed in my 18-months' notice after requesting to change from "Career Engagement" of minimum nine years to "Short Notice Engagement" when you can leave any time after eighteen months, with 18-months' notice. Effectively guaranteeing you do at least three years' service. This would mean that I will have done 6 years by the time my RN career ended.

Anyway, I used to try and get to the bank of four telephone booths under the dining hall, well before the witching hour of 6pm when the cheap rate commenced. Everyone else knew the routine and the queue for the 6pm threshold started early but they would wave in anyone stupid enough to try and call the far away regions before that and have their conversation interrupted every ten seconds with insistent beeps requiring you to insert another 10p.

I couldn't be arsed queuing up. If I wanted a longer chat, I would use the phones much later in the evening when the demand lessened. So, I used to call about quarter to six and have a short 50p chat. Duty done. I could go on the piss with a clear conscience.

On this particular evening, I sauntered up with a mug of tea in my mitt, asked if it was okay and was waved on by those at the head of the lengthening queue. Armed with five 10p pieces, I called home and was greeted by my wailing Mum. Trying to shush her cost the first two 10p's as she cried "it's all gone wrong, your Dad had gone round to pick her up."

"Pick who up?" I shout, whilst struggling to think as the fourth 10p goes in

"Beverly" shouts Mum as the final beeps go and the line goes dead. What the fuck.

I legged it up to my mess for some more change only to find that the coins I used were my last. So, grabbing my wallet I ran into the NAAFI club, who very kindly changed me a fiver without requiring me to purchase anything (normal routine) and I ran back down to the massive queue. Where my pleas of its an emergency fell on deaf ears. So, with shouts of fuck off and yeh, I've got an emergency as well, I picked up the queue from the back.

It took a long time for the queue to thin out and I could finally get onto a phone, where a much calmer Dad answered and briefed me before handing over to Beverly.

Seemed that Bev's mum Beryl had chucked her out in a dispute over who would walk her down the aisle. Bev wanted that to be her Dad but as her Mum and Dad were divorced, Beryl wanted her husband Wilf to walk her down the aisle or failing that herself. Bev said no and thought that was the end of it.

When she got home from work, Beryl had packed her bags, left them at the front door and changed the lock. Bev had rushed to the nearest call box in tears and rang our house number. Dad answered. Sussed it all out quickly and told her to wait there. Then he drove over, picked her up and brought her home.

In a strangely perceptive mood only a few weeks earlier, on a driving lesson with my Dad, I had asked him if anything ever happened, could Beverly move in with us. Dad said of course and asked why but I didn't know why I had asked. It was just a dark thought that had passed through my head. I had no other premonition, just that.

Bev moved into Hillbrook Road, taking over David's bedroom. David was at University. When we were all at home, we played a musical chairs version of beds. I had a single bed in with Ged, or David did when he was home. When we had both returned from our travels, David and I had the two single beds and Ged had a camp bed in with Mum and Dad. We made do.

By now, any opportunity to come home was taken. Lifts as far as Stoke on Trent, Sandbach or Knutsford Services and a Dad or David pick up from there. Sometimes thumbing lifts. Sometimes on the train when I felt I could afford it.

I spent a lot of weekends at home. Sneaking across the landing in the middle of the night for some physical romance.... I never kidded anyone really and we did have some chats with Mum and Dad over it.

The situation was becoming increasingly untenable, so we made the decision to accelerate our plan, buy a house as soon as we could and get married whilst I was still in the mob. So, we did.

We had saved up a lot of money. A lot for our little world anyway. However, it was never going to be enough to buy a house, pay for a wedding and have a honeymoon. So, we compromised. House and a low-cost wedding, no honeymoon.

Our first house was on Petersburg Road in Edgeley, which we bought for £10,300 after chipping the vendor down from £11,500 on account of the amount of work needed to modernise it. Bev, supported by my Mum and Dad decorated the house from top to bottom, whilst still living at Hillbrook Road. I weighed in with some odd work when I was home for weekend but the lions share was carried out by Bev.

Back at Mercury and a stroke of luck, Dave Eaton my languid mate from Timperly off the Ambuscade, had an administrative role in the "MACCO" the main administrative centre. He took my card out of the duty rolodex file and shredded it. "No more duties" he announced and there weren't.

I didn't do any more midnight patrols or have my weekends broken up by duties. Bonus. I bought him some fags and we had a few beers reminiscing about our Vegas and Barstow trip the year before in the Mercury Club. A good lad.

Born in Stockport - Grew up in the Royal Navy

We lost contact about a year or so after I left the navy, despite meeting up for beers a couple of times when we were both civvies. Dave was working for one of the tool hire companies, whilst I was working shifts at Stockport Council.

I successfully completed the four-week course and returned to Chatham for the anarchy of refit on the Soberton.

Daily treks from the accommodation blocks up on the hill, down to the dockyard, the boat and the portacabins. Sometimes Spider would give a load of us a lift in his Ford Cortina Mk1. Other times, we would just take his car and start it with a locker key and drive it ourselves. Sometimes using it to go out of the dockyard to get a Chinese takeaway when the chefs were on a particularly difficult part of their training and we needed to eat out... we still laugh about it today in our Facebook group, where we all maintain contact.

Being lazy sods, we drank in the first pub outside the dockyard gates, the less than salubrious Royal Marine, with some dubious activities we will come to in a short while.

Our ship (or boat) HMS Soberton was constructed between 1955 and 1957, completed just 5 days before I was born in September. She was commissioned into the Fishery Protection Squadron (FPS) and remained so for her entire 35-year career until February 1992, becoming the HQ for Woolwich Sea Cadets until disposal in 1998 when she was sold and broke up.

Main armament was a 40mm Bofors gun, with an assortment of GPMG's, LMG's, SLR's, Sterling sub-machine guns and browning handguns held in the armoury down below, some of which we needed to use in a number of different situations. On guard alongside at Moscow Jetty in Belfast once but mainly employed when we had to carry out armed boarding's when foreign trawlers weren't playing to the rules, more of which we will get to.

With a complement of 33 maximum, everyone pretty much knew everyone and everything that was going on. Such was life on a minesweeper. The ships company did complete a long walk to raise money for charity but I wasn't ships complement then. Team building was pretty low key and mainly consisted of trips to the boozer, wrestling with the refurbished elements of the Sobie and playing the board game "Risk" until the early hours of the morning.

As the ship fit out neared completion, we were exposed to some of the niceties of a civilian refit when the Chief Shipwright asked me what finish I would like in the Wireless Telegraphy (WT) office. I asked what were the choices? He told me they included teak, oak, pine or melamine. Wow, melamine, then the most modern of finishes that most kitchens being sold by MFI were made of. Chipboard sheet covered in plastic. So that's what we had.

Teak trimmed shelf edges made of grey melamine. A hinged glass top to our work desk with some green snooker table baize underneath it. Teak backed destruction kit board, where we stowed the hammers, chisels and axe to destroy the comms kit should the need ever arise (like we were sinking or similar...). It looked the bees knees and stirred a lot of attention amongst our peers when we re-joined the squadron post re-fit up in Rosyth but we had a few escapades before that would happen.

The civilian refit team didn't have some of the experience needed to do some of the jobs and needed our help. However, union rules meant that the dockyard workers had to carry out the task and not us. Crazy. In my case it was fitting the High Frequency aerials. Our little "main roof" of wire that enabled world-wide communications out at sea evidently.

So, there we are, like the blind leading the blind. I had never constructed one from scratch before either and had to read up on it from one of our comms bibles. I had repaired some odd bits here and there but that was it. After reading up the stuff I thought we needed, I got the gist and shared my thoughts with the Chief Shipwright, who in all honesty, had to agree with me as he had even less experience than me. Glass insulators, back spliced copper knots and serious bits of naval nuts and bolts, plus a few hundred yards of brand-new copper wire wound cables.

The test of faith was when we pulled it up under load and stretched it out. I think we were all mightily relieved that it stayed up there. Not just for the day but the rest of my time onboard. A damn fine job. I shared a pack of 200 duty free with the riggers as a mark of respect, which they responded to by buying a load of raffle tickets raising money for our ships football team kit, as we didn't have any.

I had written a letter to Sir Matt Busby asking for some of United's old kit. He wrote back to me with a lovely letter explaining why they couldn't but sent me a football signed by the then first team squad including Martin Buchan, Gordon McQueen, Steve Coppell, Gordon Hill and others including Dave Sexton the manager.

We raffled the ball for £1 a ticket. Quite a sum really but we needed to raise a lot of money. On the day of the draw, our Skipper Jonathan Band in front of a largish crowd of dockyard workers, ships company and a naval photographer.

The skipper drew out the winning raffle ticket, which had his name on it. So, he announced that wasn't fair and to a round of applause, pocketed his ticket and reached into the bucket for another. He drew out a second ticket and announced that the winner was. Me.

JB had drawn out one of my tickets. So, I thought I had better to the right and honourable thing and announced that I would return the prize for someone else to win.

The skipper then announced that as I had written the letter, arranged the raffle and sold all of the tickets, the least we could do was give the ball to me. So, he did and to a round of applause and some jeers from the docky's I took possession of the prize… haha.

I gave the ball to my little brother Ged, who still has it.

I was weekend duty one Friday and Paddy McCaig, the sub-lieutenant Corro and Mick O'Gara, the Petty Officer and Coxswain wanted to go out on a club crawl and asked me to join them on the Saturday night. They looked a bit dismayed when I rocked up in my standard going out gear of jeans, t-shirt and a leather bomber jacket. I was told that my dress code was unacceptable to the officer and senior rate who both sported suits. That, plus a choice of t-shirts was all I owned.

Born in Stockport - Grew up in the Royal Navy

The Corro loaned me a jacket, the Coxswain handed me one of his white shirts and a tie and I borrowed a pair of dark shoes from one of the dabtoes on duty. Right, we can now go ashore.

The Coxswain used to drive a metallic green 3 series BMW that went like shit off a hot shovel. He proceeded to drive us around the Kent coastline and we visited a number of large posh hotels and some clubs in Gillingham, Rochester and Chatham. The three of us drank a good eight or nine pints and Mick drove throughout. Then we went for a "Chogey Nosh" takeaway (Chinese meal) and ate it in the car.

I managed to spill a good dollop of sweet and sour chicken down the front of my nice outfit and had to cough up for dry cleaning bills for the jacket and trousers. The shirt boil washed but the tie was a write off. The night cost me a lot more than three or four rounds of beers, that's for sure.

The landlord of the Royal Marine announced that he was having a ram roast for all the locals and the ships company of the Soberton before we sailed for work up. Essentially a series of daily sailings to check everything is working, then off to fight pretend wars under the control of FOST (Flag Officer Sea Training) who had the task to make sure that a ship and its complement, were fit enough to fight and be permitted to join the fleet.

So, we get to the Royal Marine and we could smell something awful from the road outside, something burning. We got in and the story unfolded, told in part by the bar staff and some of the locals.

The landlord wanted lamb. Sadly, in short supply in the middle of winter had he bothered to ask anyone in the know, unless it came in a frozen pack from New Zealand. So, his local butcher had quoted him an expensive rate for a whole frozen lamb and he thought it would be cheaper to steal a live one, kill it and cook it.

This is of course, way ahead of Bear Grylls television programmes about survival on an island, this was a pub in the urban district of Chatham. He managed to persuade two of the locals to drive into the Kent countryside and capture a sheep. They didn't have rope, only a length of clothesline from the pub yard's washing line.

Born in Stockport - Grew up in the Royal Navy

The two guys managed to corral a sheep and brought it back to the pub in the back of a transit van. The landlord asked them where the body was and they explained that neither could kill it and it was still tied up in the outside lavvy with the washing line.

Someone went in and used the washing line to choke the sheep to death. Then they hammered a fence post through its chest and out its arse, placed it onto a makeshift pair of trestles and roasted it over a fire. Hence the smell. They had neither skinned it, nor gutted it. The wool was burning and the offal was stinking....

At the bar I was offered a chunk of red hot, partly cooked mutton, dripping with blood and fat. No thank you. Outside in the dark, lots of people seemed to be tucking in and all I could think of was it could well poison them, let alone not taste right as the frightened animal would have disgorged adrenalin all through its body as it died in panic. Thankfully, we sailed the following week and didn't frequent the pub anymore.

The work up week was a complete shock to my system. We day ran from Lowestoft and Felixstowe, steaming in straight lines, tight circles, twisting and turning. It completely wrecked me. I couldn't focus on anything other than the bleach puddled bucket I continually threw up in.

Then we were on to FOST and had to get through a series of fires, explosions, damage control exercise, mine-sweeping exercise, more fires, more explosions and were put to the test. Fire the guns, repel boarders, jump into the boats and board other things. It was incessant. Despite my limited contribution, the ships company and the Sobie were passed fit to join the fleet and we headed up the east coast to report into MCM HQ in Rosyth and then the HQ of the Fishery Protection Squadron. A squadron that had been in place for over 100 years, protecting UK fishing.

Our MCM Chief Radio Supervisor was only Alfie Marks my old RS from the Ambuscade who laughed his socks off when he saw me on the Sobie and stated that he expected me to die. Of seasickness. Thanks. Hoping you are going to die is sometimes the only thing that keeps you going when you are continually dizzy and throwing up.

I would like to say I got used to it but that would not be true as any of my shipmates would testify. I still tried to eat as much as I could, if only to stop the dry retching that hurts your stomach muscles when you try to chuck up nothing. I left the Soberton and the Royal Navy in December 1980 weighing 10st 2lbs, only a few pounds heavier than when I joined up in 1974. Not many people can say that.

Although I was over 12st at one point of my career. The minesweeper diet really worked for me....

Once we crashed and bashed our way out to sea properly, our task as part of the Fishery Protection Squadron (FPS) was to patrol all around the fishing grounds of the UK ensuring that trawlers complied with the laws of the day.

This meant boarding trawlers in the approved fishing grounds and arresting those that fished in the wrong areas or had caught the wrong fish or using illegal gear like tight gauge nets that picked up everything including fry that would never mature.

For a communicator, each boarding meant sharing the data that the boarding team collected, on notepads and by tape recording sometimes, in an admiralty signal that was sent to the Ministry of Agriculture, Fisheries and Food (MAFF), the FPS HQ and the Ministry of Defence, UK (MODUK). The most trawlers we boarded in one single day, using two boats and involving the entire ships company for the day was 23. I think the record at the time was 25 in a day. Hectic and tiring.

Each time we boarded a trawler the fishermen presented us with a basket of fish. Doesn't sound much until you realise that a basket is fourteen stone. The catch would be brought back by the boats coxswain whilst the guys on board were measuring, checking holds and recording data.

Back on board, there were only a couple of us that had the basic butchery skills and the stupidity, to wade into the mass of fish, select the good stuff and get it prepared for our freezers. The really good stuff like Dover Sole, Lobsters etc. were usually destined for the wardroom. A large chunk of Cod, Saithe, Haddock etc. would be put into our freezers and substitute for victuals, which became a great source of funds to the Soberton's social club, as fish replaced meat on a number of our weekly programme of menu's.

Fraud in all honesty but all looked on in good taste by all involved, until it got dark and serious but we will come to that.

Sometimes, we would take big blocks of frozen fish home, wrapped in a variety of coverings, if one could get home before it melted and stank out whatever source of transport had been rustled up.

The day we boarded 23 trawlers, we filled every freezer, had mammoth fish meals all day but still had to sweep loads over the side once it got dark.

Boarding a British trawler, we would be helped on board. Pulled over the gunwale and assisted on board. Not so with the French, Belgian or Spanish boats, where the crew would just stand and watch us struggle, particularly difficult when there was a heavy swell and our arrivals on occasion could be quite ungainly.

The Soberton would carry enough fuel, water and victuals (including beer) for about a week then we would have to put in somewhere to top up. Most of the time we sailed into small civilian harbours, occasionally into Rosyth and Faslane, almost never to Guzz or Pompey, which meant lots of leeway and informality that we could never enjoy in a Royal Naval base.

The Soberton would "stand down" for 24 hours usually. Sometimes for 48 hours.

JB had me draw a map of the UK and list where all the ships company lived. He would try his hardest to let the lads go home if it were feasible, from ports all over the country. If they could get home, even for a few hours, he let them go and left it to us to sort out all the duties between those who had to remain.

The guys let go home had until 15 minutes before we sailed to get back on board. Something never offered to ratings on any other warship I have ever known. It was a great routine and not one person ever let him down.

We would have "RadPhone" calls on the go all week, where we used the military radios to link into the national telephone network via set providers and let the guys talk to their loved ones at home to make arrangements to be picked up and dropped off or get a train home.

Bev and I duly tied the knot on 3rd May 1980 in a lovely church wedding at St.Albans in Offerton. I was accompanied by my best man Paul Finch, killick bunting and my bezzy oppo whom I met at Northwood, plus Smudge the Chef, Stokers Chico Hamilton and Willie Rushton with Alf Richardson (former dabtoe) from the Soberton and Gabby Hayes and Mark Eddiford, Radio Operators off the Antrim. Spider missed the celebrations following his emergency appendectomy, a fact which I have never let him forget...

Getting home for me was a nightmare, despite the small perk of extra travel warrants. As I got married in May 1980, I was immediately awarded 8 additional travel warrants a year because of my marital status. 12 free tickets. I never used more than 3 as despite patrolling within the 12-mile fishing limit, we rarely got anywhere close to where I could get home. I think I saw Bev no more than three times between May and October that year. Something we both found very difficult as newlyweds.

To be fair, we had a Short Maintenance Period (SMP) in Liverpool for ten days and the Skipper let me day run home in a car I hired. I worked 08:00 – 15:00 onboard, then tore home. Did the reverse journey the following morning at 06:00, with the weekend either side and didn't have to do any duties there. Thank you, Sir.

A rare one for me was a long weekend home from one of the few occasions we popped back into our home port of Rosyth, shortly after workup and we had been passed fit to join the rest of the fleet. It was a late finish and the choice of trains was limited. Even worse, a really bad storm had pulled the overhead lines down so the only trains running were the ones powered by diesel.

The sight of crowded platforms waiting for a train, any train, has always dismayed me and you know it is going to be hard to get home. However, get home is the intention, by whatever means.

We used to adopt a tried and tested method of travel. Get what you can when you can, going as far as you can, towards home.

Squeezing into a local, calling at all stops and lampposts between Edinburgh and Carstairs was the second leg, after a torrid wait at Inverkeithing into Edinburgh. Both trips had us resembling sardines in a can, we were only missing the tomato sauce.

A long wait at Carstairs and then another local train thing across and down to Carlisle. We missed one as we couldn't get in any door the train was that full. We got to Carlisle pretty late, three or four matelots', all with the same type of navy brown holdall's slung over our shoulders. We took advice from a kindly British Rail (BR) station supervisor who explained that the overnight sleeper to Southampton was due in. Normally all first class, it had been declassified in order to move as many people as possible. He told us to follow him over a walkway to a different platform.

Right on cue, this beautiful shiny train slid into the platform. The BR man told us all to get on and squeeze in as many people into a compartment as possible. When we got onboard, I was staggered by the plushness of the six armchair style seats in posh maroon upholstery awaiting us.

An elderly couple were shown the seats first, then we all piled in. I think we had ten or eleven in the compartment and we sat on the arms of the armchairs in between the six seats, with one other sat on the floor.

We saw more and more people on the platform all trying to squeeze onto the train and the BR supervisor shouting instructions to his team to get the doors shut so they could move the train off and get the next one in.

A largish lady and her younger female companion stood at the entrance to our compartment and announced that she had reserved seats and some people had to move out of them and off the arms in between. The elderly couple started to rise but were checked by one of the matelots who told them to remain as we had been given good advice by the BR staff.

The large lady did no more than walk down the corridor to the door, leaned out and rapped the station supervisor, who was facing away from the train, on the shoulders with her umbrella. "Young man" she snorted, "there are other kinds of people in the first-class compartment, you need to get them out."

The BR guy turned slowly and stared at her before announcing that the railway had something like twenty thousand people stuck on platforms across the north of England and we are just helping them get home. Shut up and close the window. She tried to get back inside our compartment but one of the other guys, non-matelot stood in the doorway and told them to "Fuck off". So, they did.

Other times, we were never near anyone's home and popped into some remote places for rest and recuperation. Whenever we did that, I would try and organise football matches.

Born in Stockport - Grew up in the Royal Navy

Out of a crew of no more than 33, we would often field a decent-ish 11 a-side team. I would spend the days before we landed, swapping duties around and negotiating with the senior rates on board to make it happen. Getting Smudge Tanky to buy Alf a beer to do his QM duty, or Spider to buy Willie Rushton something to eat when next alongside to cover his fuelling and watering up stuff and things like that. I was the team manager, coach, guidance counsellor, kit man and players agent all in one.

We were patrolling off the west coast of Scotland and I had made contact as per usual with the harbour master to put in our request for access to potable water and clear the jetty ready for a tanker etc. and would ask if he knew any local football teams who would play us. I really hit the jackpot for Mallaig. The harbour master was a referee in the west highland league. A level of football not known to me but as it was off season, he would have to see if he could rustle up a team. Okay and left it with him.

On our way into Mallaig we spotted an Oban based trawler that was trailing its nets into the 2-mile inshore fishing zone, a real no-no as that is where all the fry usually are, trying to grow up into fish they can then catch. So, we called him to heave to and boarded.

We found that the trawler had transgressed several different issues. We arrested its skipper and escorted it into Mallaig under armed guard, where we docked, near to four other Oban trawlers... hey up. Its nets and total catch were confiscated and a fine was expected. Therefore, no wages for the trawlers crew.

Born in Stockport - Grew up in the Royal Navy

The Skipper, Number One and Corro (Correspondence Officer) took transport with the arrested trawler skipper to a special court. The ship took on fuel, water and a few pallets of victuals and I marshalled the team up the road to a lovely little football ground where we got stuffed 6-1.

I was desperately trying to mark their striker who scored a hat trick. Turned out he was the duty police sergeant for Mallaig and we were to see a lot of each other during the evening after the game and post-match beers had ended.

Most of the wardroom was still missing and I was asked to take on Officer of the Day duties, which was okay as I was a bit brassic and wanted a quiet night in, onboard. That didn't last long though...

The wardroom steward, Ghengi (pronounced Gheng Eye), not sure of his real name but he did have some resemblance to Genghis Khan and so it was shortened to Ghengi. Anyway, his missus had written him a "Dear John" letter that he picked up in the mail bag waiting for us in Mallaig. Evidently, she had run off with his brother.

Ghengi promptly threw a wobbly and got very drunk and angry. It was decided for his own safety to strap him into a Neil Robinson (rigid) stretcher rather than lock him down our makeshift brig. It was a nice summers evening and the duty Quarter Master (QM) Able Seaman Dave Bamber (Bambi) to keep an eye on him.

Chico full of ale had arrived back on board and Bambi asked him to cover QM for a few minutes whilst he took a piss. Chico was intrigued as to why Ghengi was in the stretcher. Completely unaware of the "Dear John letter" engaged him in conversation and shared some of his supper with him. Ghengi said he was being wound up and would Chico please set him free. Chico clearly seeing the sense of it, unlatched the stretcher only to watch in horror as Ghengi threw himself over the side to drown himself. And missed.

He had jumped over the jetty side and landed heavily breaking his leg and dislocating a few things. Bambi returned, saw the empty stretcher and a bemused Chico looking over the ships side at the writhing form of Ghengi down on the jetty. Being the sober one he called for an ambulance and I had to scribble furiously a story for the ships log when I returned onboard.

Born in Stockport - Grew up in the Royal Navy

I was ashore negotiating with the duty police sergeant and the landlord of the pub just out of the harbour where Leading Seaman Matthews had smashed up the toilets following an altercation with some of the Oban trawlermen.

The landlady was screaming that it was hundreds of pounds of damage. I surveyed the scene. He had wrenched a cistern off the wall and smashed it. Water was pissing everywhere until the landlord turned it off at the stop tap. Lots of water puddling about and a smashed bit of pot.

The copper was pretty calm and insisted that I sort it out or he would have to arrest Matt for criminal damage, even though others were probably involved, they had all done a runner. I quietly asked Matt how much cash he had on him, £40. Right.

I started bargaining at £20, with the screaming landlady wanting a ridiculous £200. I asked the landlord to remove her as she wasn't helping by being so emotional and supported by the police sergeant, she was led away.

The landlord dropped to £80 and I upped to a "final" amount of £40 or the copper could arrest him, and it would take months to get any money out of Matt. The silence of the Mexican stand-off was ended when the landlord sensibly took £40 in his hand. It wouldn't have cost him that to fix it. The police sergeant drove us back to the boat, more in terms of showing he was doing his job than anything else, which is when I encountered the ambulance taking Ghengi to Accident & Emergency. The sergeant made a note, said goodnight and drove off. Fuck me it was all go but it didn't end there.

We had a new Jimmy on onboard, the second in command, or Executive Officer (XO) and we hadn't bedded him in yet to all the idiosyncrasies we had with our ships company. He had spotted the Buffer coming offshore with a bottle of vodka in his clutches. The QM woke me with the news.

I reported to the new XO and was in the process of trying to explain about the alcoholic Buffer but he wasn't having any of it. He wanted the contraband seized. So, I had to organise a search of his locker. The Buffer also suffered badly with piles and was on one of the traps in the forward heads presumably trying to curl one down as he seemed to whine a lot. He was also downing the bottle of vodka in there...

We found half a flagon of cider in his locker and numerous cans of beer, all of which were confiscated.

Due to sail the following morning, the Skipper called me into his cabin to explain the evenings events to him, including the locker search. Ghengi had to remain in hospital. I could not vouch for anything other than the Buffers locker that he didn't have any more alcohol on board. Of course, he did. As part of his empire, he had bits of store all over the boat and hid his stuff everywhere.

That summer, on the 4th of July 1980, we had our grand chase. When a French trawler was spotted illegally fishing for herring in the breeding grounds that had been clearly indicated to all fishing fleets. He had been sighted originally by an RAF Nimrod aircraft out on Maritime Patrols. We were the closest naval vessel and set off to investigate.

The French trawler skipper saw us on the horizon and as we called him on the open voice channels to heave to, decided to fuck off out into the North Sea away from us and we set off in chase. The skipper called for "full revs" and the old diesel engines thrust us along at about 15mph, just a digit or two above the trawlers maximum speed.

As we bounced along astern, the French were throwing all the herring overboard, to destroy all the evidence. Well, it was being destroyed by the mile-long wake of shitehawks feasting on the dumped catch and the skipper was in a bit of a quandary. Do we stop to gather evidence or press on to make the arrest without it?

JB called all his management team together. The officers, senior rates and leading hands. He tasked us with providing him with some options, quickly now. We disappeared to consult with our teams. Leading Seaman Matthews suggested that Able Seaman Stubbings, the only ship's diver we had onboard, was prepared to jump overboard in full diving gear and attached to a float, we could go back for him later. Stubby had climbed into his dry suit in anticipation and stood in the background looking confident. JB shook his head.

That was revised a short time later with Able Seaman Stubbings, saying he was prepared to be strapped into the rigid raider and we would lower it over the side. JB shook his head, stating the solution would not involve any of his crew "going over the side" in any form or fashion. Clearly aware of the health and safety responsibility he had to his team. There would be no death slides happening here I thought, thinking back to my exploits at Pier Cellars.

So, after a short consultation with Smudge, the baby chef, I thought that we could lower a big pan over the side, tied to a length of rope and we could scoop up some evidence. In the absence of any other suggestions, the skipper waved us on with a go ahead. Smudge the Tanky tied a length of hemp to the handle of the biggest potato pan that Smudge could produce, knotting the rope into the hole in the handle that Smudge would hang the pan up with, when it wasn't in use boiling potatoes.

All looked good as the pan was lowered into the sea but as soon as the pan filled with water, pretty instantaneous in all reality, with the speed of the Soberton, those pesky physics calculations that we didn't consider, came into effect. The pan assumed significant proportions of weight, with immediate effect, that had the rope ripping through Smudge the Tanky's ungloved hands.

He squealed as they burnt and he let go of the rope, which disappeared over the side quicker than a racing snake and Smudge the baby chef squealed "Where's my potato pan!" Probably full of herring sinking to the bottom of Dogger Bank and providing a meal for something else.

Plan B was to get a pan with holes in. Smudge's colander wasn't deemed big enough, so we grabbed the big chip fan strainer, on account the water would rush through it but there would be limited drag and we should gather evidence, and we did.

However, whilst the chip pan strainer let water pass through it, it also forced the fish through it. As we pulled up the strainer at periodic intervals, it contained fish skin, some bits of head and the odd eye and lots of watery goo.

After half an hour, we had a bucket full of chum. The sort of goo that fishermen scoop out into the water to attract sharks and similar. The skipper wasn't too impressed but it was as good as he was going to get as the French trawler ran out of herring to throw away and we closed within range of the 40mm Bofors gun.

Able Seaman Bamber (trainer and aimer) and Able Seaman Dave McFauld (loader and layer) were in their element as the Skipper issued the last verbal warning before he instructed them to fire and they did.

I cannot remember how many rounds were fired before the French trawler hove to and we prepared for an armed boarding. Which we did. The skipper placed a small detachment on board as the crew were arrested and we escorted them into Leith Harbour, Edinburgh for an evening court appearance and we all got a bonus run ashore.

The lads who boarded the trawler as the armed escort, however, were in no condition to go ashore with us as the French trawlermen had filled them with red wine, in a booze fuelled "singathon" on the way into Leith Harbour. Big Chico Hamilton for one, had to be poured into his bunk when we got alongside.

The rest of us went ashore for some big eats and ended up in a pizza place halfway between Leith Harbour and Edinburgh city centre, somewhere along Leith Road. We then marched back to the Soberton limping and whistling "Yankee Doodle Dandy" as if we were Americans celebrating Independence Day. Like you do when you are drunk on the 4th of July.

We sailed the following morning on the tide and discovered after all that effort, the French got away with resisting arrest and a fine, as the evidence of fishing for herring was legally announced as being inadmissible, and the chef had to order a new potato pan from stores. So, he had to boil potatoes with a clutch of smaller pans for the next week or so. He also boil washed and scrubbed the chip pan strainer.

In my last month or so at sea, we were due to sail on my 23rd birthday and I hadn't told anyone as I didn't want to get pissed the night before we sailed as it was a bit roughers out there. However, just as it became known it was my birthday a bit of lagging blew out of the funnel in a blast of black soot and the engines shut down. We would have to stay in Rosyth another night whilst the mechanics fixed it. Hurray went up the cheer. We can celebrate Polly's birthday.

Lunchtime we crowded into the NAAFI bar on the jetty, which opened for only 45 minutes at lunchtime, insufficient time to get pissed was the probable intent, so I slammed down a couple of pints of tartan.

Me and Brigham took the afternoon off and played "uckers "in the mess (Uckers is best described as a game of Violent Ludo) and ploughed through a crate of Heineken Export during some entertaining games. Twelve 300ml cans of lager each. At close of play, sometime around 4pm, he staggered home to see his beloved "Aggie" his lovely wife Beverley in the married quarters estate for a bonus night of nookie. I decided to turn in and was in the process of climbing into my pit when my messmates, who had just finished work, wanted to join the party.

We had a few more cans on board and I was legless. I had to be helped into the shower, dhobeyed up and dressed, then taken ashore to celebrate my birthday. The events thereafter are very hazy from my perspective. The plan was to get some "Chogey Nosh" in Inverkeithing. I had eaten breakfast but only a liquid lunch and was pretty hungry.

By 7pm, we are in a bar in Inverkeithing and I have a line of untouched pints of tartan in front of me. Another round is called in and I was asked if I would prefer a small one, nodding to the line of beers. I squinted up at the optics and the only bottle I must have focussed on was Pernod and ordered one. I necked it. It was horrible and so drank about half a pint of one of the beers stood in front of me. Get him another one was the shout. This is a good game. Give him a pernod and he sinks half a pint of beer, which is how I must have caught up on rounds.

Someone counted that I had around 27 Pernod's, most with lemonade. Followed shortly afterwards by me struggling to breathe and feeling distinctly unwell. It was decided I had drunk enough, so we didn't go to the "Chogey" but would be transported back on board in a taxi whilst everyone else went to eat. Cheers.

I do remember the QM trying to get me down below as it was evening rounds in the dockyard but I thought I would die if I went down below and fought off all attempts to placate and then drag me down the hatch. I was still fighting when dockyard rounds came and I passed out and evidently stopped breathing. I do have a memory of wearing an oxygen mask and being carried over the gangway on a stretcher. Other than that, I have no memory of having my stomach pumped or being passed fit enough to spend the rest of the night in a cell.

I do recall a lovely Joss talking to me in daylight hours. He told me that he had spoken to Mick O'Gara on the boat and that I was a good lad and particularly good Leading Hand. If I could stand up, scrub out the cell where I had been ill, he would let me go back on board without a charge. I thanked him very much and then threw up all over his trousers and boots.

The ensuing shouting and being thrown about the cell were not pleasant. Once I scrubbed it out and I really do not know how I did it. I was escorted back to the Soberton. I had to be slung between two Killick Reggies and hauled to the gangway of the Sobie down "minesweeper alley" with a crowd on each of several sweepers and my own boat cheering me on.

After being booked onboard I was slung into my pit and a watch put on me. I didn't get out of bed until the following day, when the Skipper trooped me for being Drunk Onboard. A serious breach of the Naval Discipline Act.

At the table Mick O'Gara, as the Coxswain and ships police officer read out the charge, the Correspondence Officer Paddy McCaig took notes. The Skipper demanded to know who was drinking with me. I looked at Mick who had bought me several beers and then the Corro who had started the run of Pernod's and looked straight into the Skippers eyes and lied saying "I don't remember Sir".

JB was good. He only fined me two and half days pay and let me keep my hook. Then he called a "Clear Lower Deck" and had the entire ships company on the sweep deck where he addressed them all. Giving everyone a clear bollocking that I could have died. The wrong of filling a man with ale when he has clearly had more than enough. It was not funny. It was dangerous. He went on "and if he had been a dog, he would have rolled over and died!"

I am still unclear as to the greater meaning of the dog reference but it is something my shipmates off the Soberton have never forgot and I am always reminded on the occasions we get to reunite.

Alongside in Newcastle for a thirty-six-hour stand-off (different to allow for the long time to navigate down the Tyne and match up with high tides on entry and exit), we decided to have a rig run ashore. A load of us ended up in a nightclub where one of the highlights was a limbo dancing competition. As drunk as I was, I was still pretty fit and managed to win the competition and received a bottle of Dry Cane (white rum) and a pair of towels.

Flushed with my success I staggered over to a call box and spoke to Beverly announcing that we were now in possession of two lovely towels and she hung up on me. Evidently, she didn't feel like chatting at 1 in the morning. Puff.

We did have a football match in Newcastle but had chosen opposition that was far too good for us and we ended the game early when they scored their tenth goal and we retired to their lovely clubhouse for post-match beers and outlasted their feeble attempts to match us beer for beer, for a small victory to us. Some of them tried to come out in the evening and meet up with us but they were wrecked, so we lost them, just like losing Lennie. Except we just walked out and left them slumped in the pub. Civvies. Fuck em.

The drama occurred as we were preparing for sea. Usual routine. Check fuel levels, water levels, start up the engines etc. and the Skipper was walking round checking everyone and everything was shipshape. He got to the little flat that divided the galley and the WT office and chirpily asked Smudge the Chef "What do we have for lunch today baby chef?" to which our intrepid Smudge replied holding a bag of spuds in one hand and a chicken in the other, "Not much Sir. Not sure how far one chicken and 5lb of spuds will go with 30 of us onboard."

"Where are all the vittles' baby chef?" demanded the Skipper.

"Best speak to the Coxswain Sir" replied Smudge.

So, the skipper stamps through the hatch and knocks on the Coxswains cabin door, which by now has a small audience of Smudge sticking his head out of the galley, me having pulled open the WT office door and two dabtoes hanging upside down from the wheelhouse and they must have been thinking the same as me, this will be good. And it was.

Mick O'Gara opens his cabin door looking rough in just his skidders and a floozy lay on his bunk behind him. The Skipper looks at him, looks at her and then back at Mick again and demands "Where are the vittles' Coxswain?"

Mick, the legend he was, sniffs and shrugs his shoulders and says, "Fucked if I know Sir."

At which point the Skipper blows his top and shouts his instructions "Coxswain get dressed, get that woman off my ship and report to my cabin. Corro, grab the chef and go ashore and find us some vittles'!" and that's what they did.

The incident at Newcastle began a series of events that culminated in Mick losing his job and his rate on the Soberton. The fish weren't just being used to reduce the victual cash spend for the boat, it was also being used to subsidise his shiny BMW and four houses he had bought and was renting out.

Sadly, I found out via Facebook that Mick passed away in the winter of 2019/2020, after a long and illustrious career causing mayhem as a boat skipper in the Windy's. He was a rum soul and a complete legend.

My last run ashore with the Soberton was in Grimsby, where I stayed onboard an extra day to play my last game of football for the ship and in the Navy. Bev had taken a few days off work and stayed locally in a bed and breakfast. As I left the boat for the last time, JB had one last surprise and called me into his cabin.

On his desk was a Commission Warrant and he said he would complete it now if I rescinded my notice and remained in the navy. Forgetting my drinking indiscretion in Rosyth, he said I was the sort of leader the navy needed and he would prefer it if I stayed in the mob.

It was quite an emotional moment to be honest. He must have thought a lot about me to do that and to make that offer. He did look disappointed when I thanked him profusely but went on to explain that I had made my decision. I was closing the door on my naval career and would be opening a door to my civilian career in due course.

He wished me well and off I went for a period of leave before a short week in Portsmouth, where I mustered to hand in my kit and ID card, undertake a medical, sign a shit-load of documents, then get marched off the base, no longer a member of Her Majesties Armed Forces. Quite an ignominious end when you think about it but that's how it was. I weighed 10 stone and 2lbs, just a few pounds heavier than when I joined up and half an inch taller. The minesweeper diet.

Chapter Seven

Civvy Street

After leaving the Royal Navy in December 1980, exactly 6 years and 3 days after joining up, I really struggled at first to gain meaningful employment and for a time seriously considered re-joining.

I had a recurring dream / nightmare that I was back in the mob and would wake up thinking why I wasn't in a navy bunk somewhere. Quite disorientating to say the least. The dream recurred on a less frequent basis for about ten years. Quite strange.

The option that I could return at my same rate was in place for up to 1 calendar year from discharge. However, despite a crisis of confidence as the challenge of finding sustainable employment and hopefully a new career became more difficult, I never went back.

I did some work experience (unpaid) as a labourer / driver's mate with a contractor (Denehey), who my mate Pete Ford worked for as a joiner and Phil Barrington was a driver. I did gain some useful insight into ground working during the winter of early 1981. Tough dirty work. I also accompanied an old mate of my Dad's (Frank Shenton) on a haulage distribution route as well but driving vans or lorries for a living did not seem an attractive route to be honest.

Following a lead, I picked up from the Job Centre, I did work for 45 minutes at a cheap and not so cheerful white goods retailer "Novahome" in Cheadle. Being keen, I went in early at 08:45 (start time was 09:00) and quickly sussed out the tenuous employment conditions, which differed greatly from those advertised in the Job Centre. I validated them with the shop manager and one of the owners and by 09:30 had walked out and went back to the Job Centre to complain and sign on again in a difficult meeting at the Employment Exchange.

The Employment Exchange threatened to stop my dole money for six weeks until I convinced them of the difference between what was advertised and what was in place at Novahome. Advertised as £40 per week van driver / salesman, was in fact £25 per week and the rest made up of commission on sales. The shop manager had been there the longest (9 months) and never once received a bonus. The exiting van driver / salesman, in for the day to hand over to me, actually asked me what my second job was (as this one clearly didn't support him).

When the starter motor failed and the driver had to hit the starter motor repeatedly with a hammer until it did start was probably the final straw in a mind-scrambling 45 minutes. The Employment Exchange clarified with the Job Centre that it had been mis-advertised, accepted my explanation and my dole money was not cancelled. Thankfully, a few weeks later I got an opportunity at Stockport Council and which finally got my civilian career moving.

Chapter Eight

Stockport Council

Born in Stockport - Grew up in the Royal Navy

In April 1981, I successfully navigated the selection and interview process at Stockport Metropolitan Borough Council, to start work as a Control Room Operator. Responsible for communicating with social care wardens and security teams 24/7 monitoring alarm systems, as well as providing out of hours control of all council repairs to houses, public buildings, the highway, sewers and street lighting.

Whilst things worked slowly, very slowly to what I was used to, there were many opportunities to improve things and also get into trouble...

Radio procedures were almost non-existent and often created confusion on an open audio channel, so I made some proposals based on basis radio principles in the mob but without too much of the bollocks. What I created was a fairly simple and easy to follow set of arrangements that were quickly picked up by the three hundred and odd council vans trundling round Stockport filling holes in the road and repairing houses, streetlights and unblocking sewers.

Interacting with the public again did have some funny moments... but more of that later.

When the council were still responsible for thousands of properties all over the borough, the repair line used to get inundated with calls, particularly at weekends. In the early days, we only had one operator on duty and it could be quite a handful. Almost impossible to answer all the calls when the weather conditions deteriorated and we had to receive incoming telephone calls and manage the response out there on the ground via the radio network.

My bezzy oppo Paul came out of the mob in the middle of 1981 and got a job in the RAC Control Room down the road from the town hall where I worked. He joined me at the council a year or so later. We socialised a lot with our other brother from another mother, Pete Ford who had recently left the RAF and was working as a mostly self-employed joiner. They both implored me to parade on Remembrance Day with them, as well as Pete's Dad (ex-RAF) and my Dad (ex-Army), who were also close friends.

However, I never did and still haven't because I have never felt worthy enough.

Born in Stockport - Grew up in the Royal Navy

Whilst I trained and trained, did my drills, took part in multiple exercises to practice fighting at sea and ashore. I was never required to use those skills in anger. No-one ever shot at me and I didn't shoot at anyone else, so it didn't feel right to parade with veterans who had fought in the Great War, the Second World War, Malaya, Korea, Vietnam or the Troubles in Northern Ireland.

On the 2nd of April 1982 Argentinian forces invaded the British overseas territory of the Falklands and it would have been my time if I had remained in. Almost all of my friends still serving went down south. Whilst I did receive correspondence to call me back up as a reserve, it was all over before that happened. It merely reaffirmed my stance of not being worthy.

I always remember and I always take a two-minute silence, at 11 o'clock on the 11th of November, as well as 11 o'clock on Remembrance Sunday but do so in my own time and space, never at a cenotaph or formal gathering.

In 1982 I managed to scrape up enough spare cash to buy my first car. An ancient Ford Cortina MkII 1500 side port valve tank. It had a homemade tow bar on the back that was of no real use, other than when I crashed into another car that was driving aggressively and ripped off his front and wing with it, whilst my car remained almost untouched. The resulting charge of driving without due care and attention and a £105 fine, which I had to pay off at £15 a month because I didn't have any cash, meant the cars demise and it was scrapped for a tenner from which I bought a Chinese take away for tea.

However, before that I hand painted it royal blue using coach paint, I bought from Vic Moores on the A6. I returned to see Vic when the dynamo failed and I replaced it with a re-conditioned one and then another re-conditioned one and another. Seemed that Vic Moores got a pallet of dodgy dynamos. Whatever.

Having successfully changed out the dynamo, a few weeks later the gearbox gave out its last breath and I purchased a second hand one from REMOCO, a Ford breakers yard which sold off lots of old bits off cars.

I borrowed my Dads portable drive-on ramps and used a variety of ingenious bits of wood to prop the engine whilst I removed the old gearbox and replaced it with a working second-hand version. I was mightily pleased with myself when I fired up the engine and it worked but lost the smile when I reversed off the ramps revealing four engine bolts on the road.

I couldn't work out where they went. The car seemed to drive okay and was performing well without them when I had my altercation with a Ford Capri on the A6, who had driven deliberately into my path and made me brake. I overtook him and turned left, partially destroying the front of his car with my epic home-made tow bar. The second endorsement of my career and last one, despite my efforts to improve on that score over the years.

After it was scrapped it would be a good couple of years before we could buy another car.

In 1984 we sold our terraced house for seven grand more than we paid for it four years previously and moved to a much bigger house on Northgate Road in Edgeley, that would cater for our family plans. Beverly was already pregnant when we moved in.

The big Edwardian semi-detached house had been converted and cut into two flats. I say cut because that is what someone did to the newel and handrail to the stairs. Filling the void with a studded wall and putting two door frames up, at the bottom of the stairs effectively dividing the house into two flats.

It was a requirement of the Halifax Building Society to remove the upstairs kitchen and downstairs bathroom, the dividing studded wall, and some other features before they would conclude the mortgage.

My original plan was to work on the downstairs whilst the upstairs was protected by a door, effectively sealing mum (Bev) and baby (Daniel) off from the demolition, plastering and painting. However, that opportunity had been denied us.

We also had to convert the house from two supplies of all utilities, to just one supply of each and we were not helped by some over officious and overzealous utilities representatives. The worst being the NW Gas Board who turned up, removed both gas meters, and capped both supplies…. Idiots.

It was six weeks before we got a gas supply again.

Pete Ford helped me take down the upstairs kitchen and remove the downstairs bathroom. Our Ged became my apprentice labourer work slave for his summer holidays as we took out a studded wall downstairs, the fireplaces and back boilers and carried out as much heavy building work as possible before Daniel was born. My intent was to reduce the amount of dust floating around in the atmosphere.

The midwife or health visitor came and inspected the house with the announcement that no mother or baby would be entering the worksite until the handrail on the stairs had been replaced. Great. Just at month end and I was brassic.

Pete told me about some 5" x 5" planed pine that was available, so I bought 20 foot of it, along with a load of pine planks, some heavy-duty coach screws and put up a ranch style fence as a handrail, in a temporary measure until I could get a proper job done. It lasted over 25 years and survived the three children jumping on it and climbing on it before we completed the proper job when Ged's father-in-law, Ken, a quality joiner, fitted a solid oak one.

A plumber mate of mine re-fashioned all the relatively modern copper piping into a single supply and used the excess to replace every inch of lead piping in the house. He said it wasn't a good thing to have water running through lead pipes anymore. I saw the sense in that.

The house was re-wired and I did a deal with a heating engineer from Offerton Estate called Pete McCabe who installed a central heating system.

So, by the time Daniel appeared in November 1984, after a bit of a scare, we had all new utilities connected and central heating.

Chapter Nine

Babies and Football

Bev was two weeks overdue and had been called into Stepping Hill hospital maternity wing (the baby shop) to be induced. She went into labour about ten in the evening, just after I had got home but she wouldn't let the nurses call me saying I needed some kip. They did call me at midnight, so I rose from the dead, splashed some water on my face and raced in as quick as I could. No car then, so it was the expense of a taxi.

Baby's head was stuck inside and Bev's contractions were getting more rapid. Sometime during the night electrodes were connected to monitor baby's heartbeat and mum's contractions. Bev was in and out of consciousness and I was just holding her hand providing support. So, I kind of got interested in the briefing the trainee midwife was getting from her older companion.

This dial shows mum's contractions, this dial shows baby's heartbeat. See how baby's heartbeat stops at a contraction, we call that a dip. It should then pick back up again. See? Okay I thought. If baby's heartbeat stops for two rhythms or more, we call that a type two dip and it usually means that there is some distress that we need to resolve. Okay, I thought. Though of course she wasn't speaking to me but briefing the trainee.

Sometime mid-morning the following day, the routine hadn't altered, though the staff had as the night shift went home and the morning shift started. I am holding Bev's hand and talking. A new trainee midwife is watching the kit. Hey up, I thought, a type two dip and the trainee did no more than get up and walk out, with me holding Bev's hand.

The next thing was the door burst open and medics came in all wearing green surgical gowns and asked me to get out of the way. They whipped off the electrodes, fitted a canula and put a bag of liquid that was now attached to Bev on a stand and an oxygen mask over her face and told me to move out of the way.

I didn't understand, so one of them said you should say something to her and I asked why. He replied that they were taking her for an emergency caesarean section as the baby was in distress. For once in my life, I had nothing, my heart sunk into my boots and my eyes welled up. All I could do was stick both thumbs up as a positive sign and then they were off like a team of drivers at Le Mans all running to their cars.

Bev said afterwards that she knew something was wrong when I stuck two thumbs up...

I was ushered to a small waiting room, where I broke down in tears, brought a cup of tea and left there for a long time.

A male nurse came in some time later and asked me who the hell I was and why was I in the waiting room. What?

It would seem that there had been another shift change and the morning crew forgot to brief the afternoon crew that I was still there. It took some more time to locate where Beverly and the baby was. She was in a side room in isolation. The nurse would let me look through the window in the door but not go in. Then I was sent home and told to come back at visiting time in the evening. All quite callous I think on reflection. Dad had no part in the birth, not like it is today.

It wasn't much better when Jamie was born in 1988. I could go as far as a red-line outside the operating theatre, as it was determined Bev's pelvic gap was too small for natural birth and so she had another C-Section. This time, someone in a surgical gown brought the baby out to me in the corridor for me to hold for a moment before returning him into the bowels of the hospital system. Come back tonight at visiting hours. Sounds familiar.

The birth of Nicola by C-Section in 1990 was a much more integrated method and I could sit in the operating theatre behind a green cloth screen over Bev's upper body, talk with Bev and hold her hand as Nicola was produced like a white rabbit from a magician's hat. Except she was a lot louder than a rabbit and there was no hat.

We called it a draw at three.

I had been invited to play football with a bunch of apprentices who used to meet in one of the council depots for a kick about at lunchtime. They had been organised by one of the senior electricians Jonny Angle, into a group that was playing 5 a-side on a Monday night up at Bredbury

Comprehensive School. I had no car then, so used to get a lift there whenever I could.

After football, we would go to the pub for a beer and collect subs etc. after a while I became the Treasurer and Jonny Angle was the Manager and Secretary. In 1983 we decided to take ourselves into the world of open-age football and joined the Stockport Football League. By then John was Chairman, Lawrie Martlew was Secretary and I remained Treasurer. We went from strength to strength.

We had entered a summer tournament and the organisers asked for our name so John just wrote his own name and added FC. So, we played as Angle F.C. in that first game, which we all thought was funny. However, after a beer fuelled discussion, we decided to name ourselves Metro F.C. because we all worked for the council, Stockport Met, or the Metro as we were referred to in some quarters of the town and by the police when they called us in to mop up the road after a collision, pick up fences, chop up trees that had fallen down, board up schools that had been vandalised, etc..

A sponsored 10k race brought us in quite a few quid to purchase some kit and equipment from a team that had just folded and we were off. Playing our home games at Torkington Park, Hazel Grove.

Born in Stockport - Grew up in the Royal Navy

Our first manager led us through the pre-season training, Geoff Cannon and the dad of one of our players Pete. After our second friendly match. Never quite sure why they were called "Friendlies" as they would be anything but the case. Anyway. After the second game the four us met in the pub after the game to discuss club stuff ahead of our first game of the season the following Saturday.

Geoff then announced that we had too many players in the squad. To be fair, we had around 22 players' but they were all mates and mates of mates. Geoff said that we needed to slim the squad down and left it with us to tell the players. Cheeky twat.

He had to cycle home before it got dark as he didn't drive, for some reason or other. So, we looked at the list of names he wrote down. Our best goalkeeper, our best centre half, our top-goalscoring midfielder and two full-backs, both of whom were close workmates.

Lawrie, John and I saw no logic in this move whatsoever. So, we decided to sack the Manager. John stood up and went over to the wall phone and called Geoff's home number. He must have still been pedalling home furiously when John spoke to Pete and said, "Tell your Dad he's been sacked" and hung up. So "Jangle" took up the role of team manager as well as Chairman.

I was also playing with the same bunch of lads pretty much, on a Sunday for a team called Houldsworth Villa.

When Daniel was born, Beverly announced that her and baby would be released to the world from the maternity hospital on Saturday afternoon at 2pm. However, I reminded Bev that we had a cup game that afternoon and so would arrange for my Dad to pick them up. We would have to use his car anyway as we didn't have one. Cue lots of anger and an argument about me being a proper Dad and meeting her and our new baby.

We were in dispute for two whole days but as required, I attended the maternity hospital with my Dad the driver, to receive Beverly and Daniel into the outside world. The game had been called off due to a frozen pitch.

We then introduced Daniel to the best kept building site in Stockport.

The balance between babies and football, plus working shifts was a delicate thing. I did promise Beverly that I would stop playing Sunday games when Jamie was born but we were on a magnificent run at Houldsworth Villa. We had won Division 2 of the Stockport & Cheadle Sunday League the previous season and won 12 games in a row in all competitions at the start of the 1987/88 season.

1986/87 HOULDSWORTH VILLA S & C SFL DIVISION 2 WINNERS

Therefore, I saw the season out and because we had been so successful trained and was part of the squad at the start of the 1988/89 season. However, having two little ones, working shifts and training/playing football meant everything was left to Beverly.

I was playing on a Wednesday afternoon in the police league as a ringer. Played 5 a-side Monday and Friday evenings and trained Tuesday and Wednesday evenings, shifts permitting. Playing 11 a-side for Metro FC on a Saturday afternoon and for Houldsworth on a Sunday morning. The right decision was to give some of it up. I stopped Sundays and stopped 5 a-side Mondays and most Friday's.

Born in Stockport - Grew up in the Royal Navy

After Nicola was born in 1990 Bev said that I needed to take Daniel with me on a Saturday afternoon. Shit. I thought that would cramp my style. So, aged nearly 6, Daniel came with me and I had to give him the briefing. Sat in the car. Our third car since he was born, we needed it to carry babies, bags of baby things and other paraphernalia whenever we went out as a family.

So that lunchtime, I put on his seatbelt and looked him straight in the eyes and said "What happens on a Saturday afternoon, stays on a Saturday afternoon. You will hear words you don't understand, lots of swear words, lots of stories, none of which must ever be repeated at home. If you do, you will not be able to come to football with me ever again. If you have any questions, about anything, I will always answer them truthfully but when we come home, we mention nothing about it at all. Do you understand?"

His big eyes looked at me solemnly and he said, "Yes Dad."

I thought he wouldn't last longer than one week because he never stopped talking.

Daniel loved it. He loved the banter, he loved kicking a ball about, he loved helping me with the kit bags and stuff. He was the first son to come out with us and was joined over time by about 7 or 8 others as more of the team got married and started their families off. He only stopped coming with me when he got a Saturday job aged 15...

Jamie was added to the Saturday afternoon complement when he was 5 but he was a bugger. He wouldn't stay with us, always wanting to see what was over there, running off to investigate. Bev had to agree to keep him with her and Nicola on a Saturday as it was impossible to manage or play with not knowing where he was.

By 1992 we were running three teams at Metro and were based out of the Roundhouse Pub in Heaton Norris with the chaotic couple Shirelle and Keith as mine hosts. Shirelle was known by some of our police friends as "Zorro" but we didn't really understand why in those early days. They would put on plates of ham and cheese butties, along with big plates of home-made chips. We would respond by filling the pub on a Saturday afternoon, early evening and sup a lot of ale on what was normally a quieter part of the day for them.

It was a halcyon time for us, we were playing in and winning cup finals, our first team were always in the top five of the Premier Division and we toured abroad every two years.

One Saturday evening after all three teams had won. It was party time in the Roundhouse. Daniel was running round the pub with a couple of other players sons, Mike Eastham and Nathan Billingham. They ran up to me whilst I was trying to collect match subscriptions from the players and keep my totals right when Daniel insisted, I listened to him.

Daniel: "Dad, Dad, Dad?"

Me: "Just hang on a second Danny, I am trying to add up"

Daniel: "Dad, Dad, I want to ask you something?"

Me: "I need to add this up and will be with you in a second"

One of the players, Harpo (Neil Colclough) one of my centre halves said "Daniel, your Dad is busy, let me answer your question?"

Danny looks at me and then up at Harpo and says, "What's a condom?"

Silence. Harpo tries to formulate some words and begins some shrugs and a wave of his arm, then says "Your Dad will answer that when he's finished adding up" to which all the team sat around us burst out laughing and Danny runs off with Mike and Nathan.

After the festivities we are on our way home and just half a mile short of our house Daniel recounts the moment back in the pub and reminded me of our obligations. My mind is racing and I haven't got far to drive.

"Dad, you said you would always answer my questions and today when I tried to ask you what a condom was you didn't. Harpo said he would but then said he couldn't and that you would answer after you took the subs. So, what is a condom?"

By now we have less than 600 yards to our house and fulfilling my obligation was the right thing to do, so I gave it to him straight.

"Son, when a man has sex with a woman his penis goes hard and will pass a seed onto the woman that will make a baby. A condom is like a balloon that the man puts over his penis to stop the seed from entering the woman and preventing a baby being made" was my monologue that ended as we pulled up outside our house.

I could see Daniel working this through in his head but he said nothing. I grabbed the kit bags out of the boot and together we carried them in the house. As I turned to lock the door, he was right next to me. He looked up and asked, "but why are they banana flavoured then?"

Trying not to fumble the keys I hissed "because they just are, now go and get changed!"

Brilliant. It is one of Daniel's repertoire of funny stories as he will say that he knew exactly what a condom was, he just wanted to wind me up. Yep. It worked. Well done Son. Ten out of ten. You got me.

I got a new job in 1990 working on the trams in Manchester (Metrolink) and left Stockport Council behind but not my mates, most of our players still worked there. However, Metrolink was to be a completely different level. Suffice to say that around 35% of the work force were ex-HM Armed Forces and brought with them their dark humour, insatiable drinking and get up and go attitude. All of which we will come to in due course.

Born in Stockport - Grew up in the Royal Navy

Metro FC first toured into Europe in 1990 with a chaotic and hilarious long weekend to Cologne in the then, West Germany. They didn't reunify until later that year, although the Berlin Wall had come down the previous year in 1989.

We ended the 1989/90 season with a load of honours. The SFL's annual presentation bash was at "Quaffers" one of the biggest nightclubs in Greater Manchester. The middle of the stage was like a lift on an aircraft carrier and to the sound of the "Thunderbirds" theme music would rise from the depths of the club with the entertainment already stood on it and ready to go. In the case of our league do, it was tables covered in trophies and loads of them were ours!

We had bought 84 tickets to the Thursday evening do and had lots of tables with Metro players, wives and girlfriends and oppo's sat around to receive the awards. However, the evening also clashed with our planned trip to Germany. Only seventeen of us could make the trip...

The arrangements were simple. Collect the gongs, grab some nosh and hand over the WAG's to our family and friends to escort home at the end of festivities and seventeen of us climbed into a mini coach with crates of beer and left for Germany at 22:30 to catch the right ferries the following morning.

Pete Ford had prepared a special porn movie for the VHS player and small screen on the bus. He had used a four-hour tape and copied it back-to-back with two VHS players he had, to create our four-hour extravaganza of filth. Its quality was dubious. The first two hours were okay, in full colour and sound. By the third hour, the colour went and the last hour had no sound. So, Pete grabbed the drivers microphone and mimicked his own voice overs to the action, which was hilarious. "You know you want it!" Nobody slept on the way down to the ferry port at Dover.

Pete also insisted on singing the only song he knew the words to. Buddy Holly's "It Doesn't Matter Anymore" whilst he encouraged us to sing the last line of each verse and its chorus. Pete always started at verse three (shown here as the first) and we all had to make sure we joined in "Well you go your way and I'll go mine" Brilliant. We were all brainwashed over the course of the weekend it became our tour song.

> Well, you go your way and I'll go mine
> Now and forever till the end of time
> I'll find somebody new, and baby, well say we're through
> And you won't matter anymore
>
> There's no use in me-a-cryin'
> I've done everything and now I'm sick of trying
> I've thrown away my nights
> And wasted all my days over you

When we got to Cologne on the Friday afternoon, we were introduced to a local beer called Kolsch, traditionally served in what we called test tubes, long cylindrical glasses with less than half a pint in them on account of the various strengths available, some of which was as high as 11%. Rocket fuel.

S.C. Koln-Mulheim were our adversaries on the Saturday. They had a lovely ground but we were forced to play on a redgrar pitch as a team higher in the hierarchy of local football had a game on the big grass one.

Born in Stockport - Grew up in the Royal Navy

We managed a creditable 3-3 draw and Mulheim put on two small barrels of Kolsch for our post-match drinks. My high school German somehow qualified me as our interpreter for the weekend…. Great. Not one of our hosts spoke English.

They suggested we lose the coach back at the hotel as they planned to take us onto a "Strassen Messe" or Street Fair to us foreigners. So, we did. The driver came back out drinking with us in an anarchic evening in Cologne.

After we drank the two barrels, the club arranged lifts in a variety of cars and vans. The street and town square where the party was, had been closed off and every bar had barrels outside coughing up free beer. We were in our element. Within an hour or so I was absolutely legless and stood drinking with Mulheims coach, a big guy named Rolf who started yappering at me frantically and it was a while before Mr Butcher's finest got the gist of what he was saying. The team had scattered around the street fair bars and couldn't be found. Shit. We needed to round them up and get them ready to return to the hotel.

There was a big stage in the middle of the town square surrounded by lots of tables, parasols and drinkers. Entertainment on the stage was a mixture of oompah bands and folk music. In a gap between acts, I heard the familiar words and dulcet tones of my mate Pete. He had grabbed the microphone and started singing "You go your way and I'll go mine" and as it boomed around the square, I saw Harpo stand up and join in. Then Gaz Eastham, Mick McGreevy and Dougie Wild, in a Flash Mob moment that we didn't know anything about in those days.

The Germans loved it and thought we were some kind of act. So, we all got ushered up onto the stage as backing vocals to Pete. They encouraged him to sing another one but he didn't really know any more and sang the same song again, this time with us all pitching in and a lot of the crowd joined in with us too. Brilliant. It also helped gather us all together and allow Rolf to organise lifts for all of us back to our hotel. They were terrific hosts.

Saturday was a day off as the travel agents purporting to be football people failed to secure us a game, which in one way was okay and not so in another. We instead took a trip to a theme park called Phantasialand and had a great day drinking beer, firing guns, drinking more beer and getting ill on rides.

The drinking continued in the locale around the hotel. George and Pete made their way back to the hotel with Pete in the lead. Once he had got his sleeping beacon on, he used to just head to his bed. Never told a soul. He would just take off.

As George got to the hotel, he noted a load of cotton fabric that had caught on the aluminium frame of the entrance door. It disappeared off in a straight line and followed the same route George was walking back to his room. The cotton was taut and jammed at the bedroom door. All became apparent in the morning when Pete wailed that is best shell suit bottoms were ruined, as they had frayed all the way up to shin level.

The following day was hectic and not good for our hangovers. We had a game at a German army camp and then were to head back to the ports for the ferry and long journey back up to Stockport from the coast. There was time for the Germans to host us post-match, something guaranteed by the travel agent. However, our mini-bus driver got lost.

We didn't get to the ground until late, about the time the game should have ended. We were all a little worse for wear and our little faces lost all hope as we navigated the armed guards and anti-tank chicane at the entrance and took a look at our opposition. All over 6' tall and looking fit and tanned.

Born in Stockport - Grew up in the Royal Navy

As the bus pulled up and the 17 pasty faced drunks fell out, some carrying beer, they must have realised that we were unlikely to provide them with stiff opposition. Though for the first 45 minutes, we did just that. We worked our little socks off and held them to just 0-1 at half time.

We didn't have any oranges and the Germans tank engineers must have smirked as they heard the hiss and spurt of beer cans being opened and fags lit for our half time refreshments.

In a game of two halves, we lost any vestige of energy and the army team thumped in another 6 goals before Tony Graham decided to score an own goal from one of their corners. As it floated in, he screamed "OWN GOAL" and thumped an unstoppable header past Phil Stelfox, surely the smallest goalkeeper in the world and stunned the Germans. We all fell about laughing.

The game finished at 8-0. We got showered and changed and had about 30 minutes to take advantage of a superb buffet and beer set up created by our hosts. They gave us loads of cans of beer (like we needed it) and cramming butties and chicken drumsticks into our gobs we responded to the frantic gestures being made by our wayward mini-bus driver and took off to make his ferry time.

In the coach on the way home, we reminisced greatly about a fantastic and funny weekend. Gaz Eastham was convinced that one of the forwards ran round him like Franz Klammer and he couldn't even kick him he was that fast. Some bright spark reminded Gaz that Franz was Austrian and a skier not a German footballer. To great laughs Gaz replied that would be right as the twat slalomed past him!

Back in Stockport, one our competitors, a young team that included a current crop of apprentices at Stockport Council and some other damn fine footballers who went on to get paid to play, were also based at Torkington Park but a division below us. Grove Celtic. There was some tension and a lot of banter between our first team and them, partly because of the work connection but a lot because we were competitors for the same playing pool.

We got drawn together in the quarter final of our league cup for Premier and First Division sides, The Presidents Cup. Which we won in 1990 and

1991, losing in the final of 1992 which would have been an unprecedented third time in succession.

As a club we were short of players that weekend and rather than go to our respective games with bare elevens, we drafted in some ringers. I brought in Phil McQuade. A good footballer but who had an incredibly angry streak in him. He had been previously banned for deliberately kicking a fellow club player in the head during a training session. Could have killed him but it didn't.

Phil had the dubious distinction of being the first ever Metro FC player to get a red card. It was in a game against Hempshaw Lane, with a big fat referee who never left the centre circle. He failed to spot the opposing player five or ten yards offside who ran in to score. Phil ran up to the referee and shouted, "He was offside you fucking wanker?" to which the referee held up a red card and sent him off.

The paperwork arrived from the FA and we did consider an appeal, would have been dubious but decided not to as the wording in the report stated "I was in a good position to see the Hempshaw Lane player score a good goal from an onside position. The above-named player, Mr Philip McQuade then ran up to me and shouted "He was offside you fucking wanker?" so I sent him from the field of play. Hard to argue with it really.

I got a bit of stick from the Bailey Brothers, Chris and Darren, of Grove Celtic, whom both worked for the council and knew Phil, who also used to, that it would only cause trouble if I picked him. Right, I thought, a bit of Alex Ferguson mind tricks won't do any harm. Having him on the bench would be good thing.

As it was, it was a pretty close affair but not one for the faint hearted as players were crunching into tackles all over the pitch and it was all square at 2-2 after 90 minutes and we went into extra time. I wanted to jazz things up and so replaced one of our tiring midfielders with the eager-to-get-into-the-fray McQuade.

I could see the looks on some of the Grove Celtic players as Phil gave his name to the referee. The first challenge Phil did was a monstrous and clean, block tackle on a lad called Sherratt. Who incensed, for reasons known only to him, jumped up and punched Phil, who did not fall over and did no more than punch him back and drop him. Another of their players, Edro (can't remember his full name) then leaped on Phil, so Phil decked him as well. Cue pandemonium as both teams clashed in a series of scuffles and huddles.

The referee brought the scuffles to a halt with some effective blasts of his whistle and promptly sent off Sherratt, Edro and McQuade for fighting. Cue lots of hurled insults and threats. Our ten players scored two more goals in extra time against their nine and we ran out winners and proceeded into yet another semi-final.

As we were congratulating ourselves both Baileys ran over to me and said I was going to get battered as they had warned me not field Phil McQuade.

Grabbing all the kit bags and ushering our Danny into the car where I left my spectacles, I marched into the changing rooms. I took my coat off and hung it up in our dressing room and realised I still had a watch on. Best remove it and put into my pocket.

One of our top goal scorers Dave Eastham (George) asked me what I was doing and so I told him, preparing to fight. So, George pushed me out of the way and stormed into the passageway to sort things out. We heard him shriek and fall flat on his back and I heard a voice say they've hit George and rushed out into the passageway closely followed by the whole team.

They had surged out of their dressing room as I pulled my fist back to throw a punch but the seething mass of both teams caused a serious log jam of people crammed together, some trying to hold onto each other's shirts. I had the only free arm. So, I randomly punched every face I could in the vicinity of my swing for a good thirty seconds until the logjam was broke up.

Partly with the arrival of our second team who had been playing on the pitch right outside the dressing rooms and big Dave Slater came in with a flying kung-fu kick that scattered them. It was carnage as we all continued to throw as many punches before the brawl was unravelled by lads from other teams.

Born in Stockport - Grew up in the Royal Navy

As we retired to our respective dressing rooms, someone picked up George and we demanded to know who had hit him to start off this mass brawl. No-one he said, my studs slipped on the mud outside causing me to upend myself. Fuck sake.

There was a lot of animosity around for a long while. In a funny world, Chris Bailey played for me for about 3 years later after Grove Celtic folded, after we had all made friends and got over things. Not everyone did though.

We made a decision to move from playing football at Torkington Park to the much better pitches at the University of Manchester sports ground, Willenhall Road, Northenden and a few years later, left the Stockport Football League for a new challenge with the Lancashire & Cheshire Amateur Football League (L&CAFL).

In 1992 Metro FC toured Belgium. I had worked there in my first few months at Metrolink and really took to the Belgian people and their vast range of good beers. However, we found out the day before we left, that we couldn't play any games in Belgium and would have to travel over the border into Holland. Didn't seem a problem when it's put like that.

In reality, we had long coach journey's and a ferry ride, of two to four hours on each of the Saturday and Sunday. On the Saturday we played in a very tough game against a particularly good team and lost 4-3 but had a fantastic time drinking with the Dutch in their fabulous clubhouse.

Some of the lads went back outside to have a penalty shoot out to resolve some argument or other and played strip penalty shootout. Every time someone scored, out lunatic goalkeeper Les Birkhead removed an article of clothing, eventually stood naked apart from his football boots, which attracted a large crowd of the Dutch players WAG's as Les was more than a little well-endowed.

On the Sunday, instead of a game, there was a mini-competition of 15-minute each way games. We finished runners-up and the Dutch organisers said that we couldn't have the runners-up trophy as it was worth a bit and they didn't trust us to return it, so they replaced the trophy with three crates of beer. Bonus.

Born in Stockport - Grew up in the Royal Navy

On the way back to Belgium we stopped for Big Eats at McDonald's. One of our players, Big Wayne Jones, became an eating legend. Sweet left foot but slow on the pitch, when he was running it looked like he was going backwards. However, the lad could eat. He got back on the coach and asked if anyone had eaten the apple turnover, as he wanted to know what it tasted like? It was the only thing on the menu he didn't eat. He couldn't fit it in after scoffing a Big Mac, a Quarter Pounder, a Fillet of Fish, a dozen chicken nuggets and two large portions of fries, with a large milkshake.

Before we got to the ferry port, we ducked into a hypermarket to buy as many crates of cheap beer as we could afford and also fit into the coach and there were hundreds, Big Wayne walked around the hypermarket and ate a full cooked chicken he picked up in the first aisle and left the remains in a bag on a shelf without paying for it. Jesus he could eat.

Hotel Thierry didn't really like us that weekend. It didn't help that some of the rooms had balcony's that led out onto the roof. As tour organiser, my name was already in their sights. As we were unpacking the hotel owners, sour faced individuals came to my room and gave me a bollocking about people on the roof of the hotel. Just then Brokky (Steve Brokenbrow) jumped onto our balcony and shouted "All because the lady loves Milk Tray…" saw the owners and jumped off the balcony back onto the roof and as all faces turned to me, I said "I've never seen him before in my life."

It continued the following morning before we set off for our first game, when I was led around the hotel by the owners pointing out all the indiscretions carried out by my players. Hard to argue with the puddle of beer under Choccy's bunk bed and the empty beer can sat on its side or the pee-stained mattress lay on its side drying in Brokky and Dimes room. I argued that the piss stain on the wall of the landing could have been made by any of the hotel's occupants didn't get far when she said it is only filled with your footballers.

I held the club kitty as having done this thing before, knew there would be breakages. I had just over £300 and was debating making them an offer when one of the fullbacks Briggsy slid past us holding some form of Belgian bleach in a bottle under his arm. I didn't ask. As we left for our final set of games and more beer, I left it with the owners to calculate what the damages would cost.

It seemed that someone had got up in the middle of the night in the Briggsy, Pete Leach and Col Finch bedroom, poohed in the shower (wrong foreign country for toilets like that) must have turned round a few times looking for bog roll and then walked it into the carpet getting back into bed. Briggsy had tried to clean it off with bleach and burnt white marks into the carpet instead....

The day of departure and the hotel owners were demanding £500 in whatever currency it was, either Belgian Francs or Euro's, I don't recall. I do know they threatened us with the police. I started at about £150 and we met in the middle, sort of, where I needed it to be £300. Honours even, we departed the sea-side town of Blankenberge and went home.

Unloading the piles of beer crates outside the Roundhouse when we arrived caused quite a stir. We had about ten crates each, some had more.

The 1994 football tour was to France. It was yet another hilarious and fun filled weekend that began with breakfast in the Pub at 04:00 on the Friday. Keith the Landlord, Pete Ford, Lea Harrison my ex-Army oppo who worked with me at Metrolink and Gary Billingham, first team captain. We were joined later by the rest and the coach departed at about 07:30 with most of us bladdered already and we had crates of ale on the bus to take with us.

We drank all day, played 3-card brag at all three tables on the coach, then caught the ferry over the channel in the afternoon, stopping off at a hypermarket to top up on alcohol before playing our first game that evening.

Amazingly, we managed to draw. I went on as a substitute but couldn't really see much. I saw even less when I tried to head a ball and fell flat on my back looking up at silhouettes of players and officials making sure I hadn't died.

Pete Ford acting as first aider, ran onto the pitch with a bottle of whisky and started to pour it down my neck as if it were some kind of magic elixir! Here, he said, this will make you feel better. Cue lots of laughter from our team and horrified looks from the French, who just didn't understand why we would even consider playing a game when we were drunk, let alone topping up during the match.

I was asked to leave the field by the referee and it did seem a sensible thing to do, plus I had got a taste for the whisky. So, Pete and I had a few more drams as the game petered out as a draw. Then we went to their bar for more beers and a snack before the coach took us to our hotel and out onto the town.

Saturday was more of the same. We took on a mixed-age veteran's team at a lovely little ground with a wooden pavilion. The only problem was the weather. It had been pouring down all morning and was coming down in stair rods as we filled our little changing room in the wooden pavilion.

Not all the players attended either, as a load of them wanted to watch Man United stuff Chelsea 4-0 in the very wet FA Cup Final, so we ended up with two goalkeepers and Roundhouse landlord Keith, in the squad of fourteen.

A small group of lads got changed and went out to warm up. Phil McQuade had strolled around the clubhouse and was stunned when he saw their honours boards showing virtually every team at the top of their respective tables. He scurried back to give us the bad news and asked what the worst score was we had lost on tour. Someone said it was the 8-0 drubbing by the German Army team near Dusseldorf in 1990. So that was our target, as we all opened a can of Stella Artois each and mused over keeping the score down below 7...

Phil started humming the match of the day tune and it was picked up by others, clearly enthused by the amber nectar being consumed and raised our voices with a series of punctuated "Der, Der, Der's" to the tune, supping more beer and then stamping our feet to the tune and getting louder and louder.

Outside, the guys warming up and been playing "centering and heading" just crossing balls from near the corner flag, to head in the goal and big Woodsy had done a diving header at the side of the goals and slid into a massive puddle and skidded along for about twenty feet. So, the rest of them joined in. They were already wet anyway and proceeded to run to the touchline and take gigantic swallow dives into the puddle and skid along.

The French team were stood on the wooden balcony watching the Woodsy's, Matty Ford, Harrison and others then must have heard us singing and stamping and looked in on us in our drunken dancing and must have wondered what the hell they had let themselves in for... we won the match 10-1. They were shit scared of coming anywhere near us.

To be fair, they hosted us well afterwards and we stayed for beers, cheese and ham baguettes and had a laugh over our drunken antics with them. They also let us use the clubhouse telephone to call home, which was a nice touch. I was always under strict instructions from Bev. Don't try to speak to me when you are pissed. So, I didn't.

The last full day of the tour and the weather changed to proper summer. Blue skies and a big bright sun beaming down. So, we decided to go to the beach.

Piling up the jumpers, well tracky tops, football holdalls and other paraphernalia, we made up two sets of goals and divided up into two teams for a game of beach football, watched by a number of bemused French beachgoers. As it had got hotter, we played skins versus shirts and it was then that we understood why Shirelle was nicknamed Zorro.

As Keith took of his t-shirt, we could all see that his chest and back was criss-crossed with a series of slash wounds that must have been repaired in a home-made fashion. Everyone stopped to gawp at him but he wasn't bothered and kept on playing.

Evidently, he and Shirelle would get drunk, get angry with each other and fight. On many occasions it would seem that Shirelle slashed him with a knife and then would be full of remorse and put sticking plaster or gaffer tape over the wounds. Some of the more serious ones clearly required attendance at A&E and must have been where the police got involved and how she got her nickname. Zorro.

One day in December we rocked up at the pub after our games and saw them both looking like wounded soldiers from the trenches. He had a forearm in plaster and she had a big dressing round her head. Seemed in a drunken argument, she had stabbed him through the forearm with a butter knife, severing tendons and he had bottled her in retaliation. FFS.

Their demise came about as revenues began to fall. In no way linked to her erratic style of management and mass banning of anyone who didn't agree with Shirelles point of view. They owed a massive brewery debt and decided to maximise their cash on a last night binge party, then did a runner with the cash having sold almost everything in the pub. Including the dart boards, sound system, whole barrels of beer and DJ system all owned by the brewery.

Metro FC kept continued to be based at The Roundhouse (under various new managements) until we merged with Burnage High School Old Boys (BHSOB) in 2002 to form Burnage Metro F.C. and commenced drinking beer in our own bar.

The guys in charge of the teams kept the club going for the time I was over in Australia and sadly, my old friend John Angle lost a long battle against throat cancer and passed away. I wasn't able to get home for the funeral but our Ged, who worked with him as an electrician at the council and my Dad represented me at the service and wake.

We now ran five teams on a Saturday afternoon, all playing in the L&CAFL but also had a clubhouse and football pitches to manage, a much more involved and complicated package in a 50/50 share with Didsbury Toc H Rugby Football Club. A relationship that wavered between serious distaste and outright hostilities that needs some explanation we will come to later.

The last tour that I went on and didn't organise, was the Burnage Metro FC tour to Prague. We only played one game thankfully and got battered 8-2. I managed to create controversy with a particularly late challenge that still gets views and gasps on YouTube.

Our Ged had been to Prague before and took us on the tour round but made it via a number of different bars. The lovely view from the U-Hotel roof bar being the best and a variety of other venues around the city on the tour. It was a hot sunny day and we were sinking quite a few beers.

Born in Stockport - Grew up in the Royal Navy

We got to a little courtyard and instead of beer, Lea Harrison decided that he would have a brandy. The barman brought him a little menu to choose from. Lea duly selected one and the barman returned with a massive brandy glass, a bottle and a contraption, all on a tray.

He showed Lea the bottle. Then poured a massive dollop into the glass. Then he placed the glass into a stand which had the glass at an angle. Under the bowl of the glass, the barman then put a little candle and lit it. Then he slowly turned the glass over the flame until the brandy was nice and hot, he touched the edge of the brandy to the rim, which briefly ignited the brandy then he handed it to Lea, who wisely blew out the flame and was about to neck it when I shouted "STOP" and he did.

The entire courtyard of thirty or forty people were watching and I said "It's a show, so show off" and he did. Lea rolled the brandy round the glass in some grand gesture, raised it to his lips and sipped and said "Magnifique" to the barman, who nodded his head, clicked his heels and made off with the tray and all the makings. People all round the courtyard were putting their hands up and all wanted the same. It was funny. Lea made the brandy last a while and we got a free round of shots from the barman who gave Lea a wink and a nod as he served us. Our little show must have upped his takings for the afternoon.

We carried on our grand pub crawl and went underground to yet another titty bar. The place is full of them. After a while, watching a semi-naked woman (they just wear thongs or panties) gyrating up and down or around a pole gets a tad boring. You will only understand if you've been there. So, we were just chatting and telling jokes whilst the pole bar dancing is going on in front of us, or behind us, whatever the layout was in the place we were drinking.

This underground one, was at least two floors under the road level and quite cool, which was nice after waltzing round on such a hot day. We sat at eye level with the stage and below us, were a small group of Scandinavian guys, all looking up at the girls.

The routine seemed to be one girl on the pole, one girl warming down before stepping off the stage and a third girl warming up as she just got on the stage at the T bar end. A fairly repetitive process. Ged was just remarking on a cleanliness matter and wondered if the pole was wiped down at periodic intervals with something like wet wipes, which already had us giggling when disaster struck.

One of the girls walking off the stage (warm down) was having a chat (in Czech) with the girl throwing herself at the pole. Perhaps they were deciding what to have for lunch or putting in an early request for a medi-wipe, who knew, we didn't because we couldn't speak Czech. At this moment, one of the Scandinavians stood up and must have been asking his mates what they wanted to drink. It was an assumption as they all had empty glasses but were speaking in a different language that we also didn't understand.

At that moment, the pole dancer, who was wearing some quite fetching shiny thigh length boots, swung round and the platform sole of one of the boots struck the big Scandinavian guy and he dropped to the floor like someone had shot him.

Everyone stopped. The girl on the pole was distraught. The Scandinavians were trying to pick up their friend and we were sort of watching and hoping for the best. And it was. The big Scandinavian jumped up a bit groggily and sporting a wound on his temple. The pole dancer was bent over to him offering her apologies and a big bouncer announced free drinks for everyone, which was a bonus. Then with everyone laughing and pointing, the girls got on with the show and we had another beer but it was Freemans.

Chapter Ten

Stockport Council Control Room and the Orange Cab Company

Dovetailing working shifts in the Control Room, training and player/manager with Metro FC and looking after our three children created a full on, 24/7 level of activity for me and Bev shouldered a lot more of the family stuff than I ever did.

When we could get out as a family, we did. School holidays were always full of long walks along the canal banks in Marple, down to Roman Lakes and exploring Etherow Park. Low-cost days out and often with my Mum and Dad, who adored walking. We would take a picnic of sandwiches and drinks that we consumed at specific stopping points. Great family fun and just the thing when you don't have any money and need to keep children entertained.

The Control Room though, was another world at times. I worked there for just over ten years.

It wasn't all sweetness and light in the early days until I got my head around things and I did want to improve myself and do better. I did apply to GCHQ the centre for all the governments sneaky beaky communications and was invited down to Bletchley for 36 hours to complete a series of tests.

I passed all the exams, an English paper, a Maths paper, a grilling of a panel interview but failed to master Morse code at 22 words per minute. Easy enough when I was on the Soberton, doing it every day but after a two-year layoff found it hard to stay with the speed and thus compromised my accuracy. Not helped when the "biffer" was in Portuguese, making it exceedingly difficult to fill in the missing letters as I didn't understand the language.

At the end of the day, I was called to one side and informed that I had passed everything except for the Morse code test and would I like to sit another one. Yes, I would and jumped at the chance of a reprieve. The second biffer was in Spanish and I fared no better than the first time.

I was informed that I could not apply again for six months and to "boff up" in the meantime. However, there was no opportunity for me to do that as far as I could see and gave up on my desires to be a radio spy for the government and concentrated on making it with the council.

I utilised the Orange Cab Company (OCC) for all the lifts I needed in the early days when we didn't have a car. I gave the nickname OCC to the fleet of council vehicles that were painted orange, with brown roofs and equipped with the 1980's Stockport Council logo that looked like a slanted swastika in white painted on all sides, whenever I could.

Someone would always pick me up and drop me off where I needed to go as I got known by almost all the guys and girls working across town in the different departments. Sometimes I would put a call out on the radio, much like taxi controllers do, need a pickup from the town hall going to Edgeley. Rarely walked home from an early shift.

It was one of those things that during office hours, strict demarcation lines were in place and trades were not permitted to cross each-others paths or support them but out of hours when our Control Room managed all the calls, I had all sorts of teams supporting each other to get the job done. For those on call, there was always work and that was extra bunce for the guys and girls. I helped them and so they helped me but it wasn't always like that.

I was on duty one afternoon and could hear the works traffic on the open channel radio we had and was able to track events by monitoring the chit chat. Something we were taught to do as radio operators. Listen, analyse, record and use the information gathered.

The same address came up several times, as a blocked toilet and a blocked sewer. The plumber had attended and rodded the loo then reported it was a blocked main. The sewer crew attended and jetted the main, then announced the problem was on the building maintenance side and required the plumber to re-attend. He did and rodded the loo again.

The householder called after 16:00 after all the depot lines and works control were handing over to us for the out-of-hours service, complaining that the toilet was backed up again and I listened patiently to his continued exasperation with the council. I took the call and said I would sort it.

I contacted the highways on call and the duty plumber and suggested (I was not supposed to instruct evidently but I soon changed all that crap) that they meet at the house and work on the job together, so they could determine exactly where the blockage was. Turned out to be a collapsed drain on the fence line to the house, which required a dig. The point was, they collaborated and sorted it out.

That became my ethos for out-of-hours, work the problems through and solve them by working collaboratively with all concerned. Something I was so used to doing in the Royal Navy. Work together to get things done.

My "piece de resistance" was the winter storm of 1987 after Michael Fish confidently forecast that the rumours of a hurricane hitting the UK were false. The storm with winds of up to 115mph, left hundreds of thousands of homes without power, killing 18 people and causing over 15 million trees to blow down.

I was being overwhelmed by the number of calls coming into the control room that night. With windows smashed, advertising hoardings and hundreds of trees down blocking roads and tiles blowing off roofs. It was mad.

I had called out virtually every duty trade we had on a variety of jobs but dealing with tree's down was probably the most difficult. We had both arboriculture teams out with chainsaws cutting up tree's and I persuaded them and the highways teams to merge and create four teams, one person cutting and one person acting as lookout-cum-labourer. Backing them up were a number of other highways teams using lorries with towing capabilities to haul big pieces of cut tree out of the way.

I used a road map on the wall as my key and marked it up with felt pen, which road was reported blocked, how big the tree was etc. and then despatched the crews to where I felt they were best needed.

The following year I received a letter of commendation from the leader of the council, on how I had calmly managed the response to a fire in a tower block in Brinnington, that required an evacuation and setting up of an emergency relief centre with social services, along with the building inspector and trades to make safe the building after the fire service did their bits.

There were other opportunities for me to put my marker down and had already been promoted to Senior Control Room Operator for using my initiative and getting things sorted out. For instance, I insisted on using a pro-forma message pad to record calls, show who they had been allocated to and what action was being taken. Believe it or not, there had been almost no form of record keeping previously and it beggared belief we ran on bits of notepad and a logbook. The call logs were held until the next working day when they were posted out to whichever part of the Works Division was responsible for that particular asset. The emergency responses and those we held back deemed not urgent and for the depot clerks to sort out. However, there were also a number of very silly moments...

When it was all going like a chip shop on a Friday night, it was hard to keep track of all what was going on. The message pads were being filled in and I would try my damndest to create little pockets of time to get the calls out to the on-call teams to respond to the jobs. A phone tucked in a shoulder, right handwriting and left hand clicking the Press To Talk (PTT) button on the radio microphone to alert the teams and pass on the information. Sometimes I made mistakes.

Moz: "Stockport Council Emergencies, how can I help you?"

Caller: "We are in the middle of a funeral and the sink is leaking, we need help?"

Moz: "With the funeral or the sink?"

Caller: ... silence....

Moz: "I am so sorry, I got a bit carried away with myself there, it's a bit mad in here today. Can we start again?"

Caller: "Yes"

Moz: "Stockport Council Emergencies, how can I help you?"

Caller: "We have a leaking sink"

Moz: "Let me get that logged and see if we can get a plumber to attend, what is your address....."

Another time in the middle of a very busy morning a lady called to say she had a dead goat in her garden... I did my best to explain that dead animals were not an emergency and should be reported to refuse collection, who did not work out of normal office hours. Then she announced it wasn't her goat but it belonged to her neighbour. I said she needed to go and speak with her neighbour then. She said that she didn't speak with her neighbour after they fell out over something.

The little display of calls was showing full with six people calling in and I tried to hurry her up by asking here to go and talk with her neighbour and sort it out. She hung up and I carried on taking calls and using the radio.

In between a large pothole in a road and a school that needed a dozen windows boarding up, I took a call and a lady just said, "She told me to fuck off" and I thought what the hell, before connecting her voice to the lady with the dead goat in her garden. So, I asked her to explain again and she repeated the message that evidently been provided via a letterbox conversation.

So, I told her to throw the goat over the fence and into her neighbour's garden. "It's too big" she wailed, so I told her to get a shovel, chop it up and throw the pieces over the garden fence! At which point, she hung up.

I expected the worst and later on that shift received a call from her local councillor, who though sympathised with me, thought my suggestion of a shovel a little too harsh. To which I agreed. We ended the call amiably when I said it was logged for refuse collection first thing on Monday morning.

We were monitoring telemetry calls on a social alarm system for the elderly and security systems in schools and public buildings. Each part of Stockport had been divided up into areas and single operator warden would respond to the social alarm calls from the elderly who had fallen over, felt really ill or needed the kettle putting on and a natter.

Security teams operated on a similar area programme but involved two-man teams that responded to alarms, reports of vandalism and anti-social behaviour in parks and other council owned property. Of course, in those days it wasn't termed as anti-social behaviour. The perpetrators were referred to as Scally's, vandals and thugs. That's generally how they got recorded into the various logs, call sheets and reports.

Shift changeovers were always a busy time, as the Wardens met to hand over their big bag of jailors keys and code numbers (no addresses) for each property to provide them with rapid access and the security guards brought their vans in. We were based in the area around the loading bay in Stopford House, tucked in behind Ponsonby House and the old town hall. It was quite secluded.

Early on in our reign, some inquisitive police came and visited the Control Room and I remember playing host and brewing up. Good to have the police on your side was my limited experience at that time of my life and they did.

PC's Pete Roden (nicknamed The Rat) and Gary Wood were the two that frequented the most. They usually operated the lock up van and both being big lads, must have been used as the last resort when it was kicking off and scally's needed arresting. Been there, done that, got the t-shirt.

The night shift was always quieter and they would come in for a late bite to eat with us, often with some shared cooking and a few beers if they had been given any on their tour of duty. We would scoff and play darts in the little rest area that had the kettle, little stove and microwave.

Gary Wood persuaded me and Brokky to turn out as ringers for his Dad's team. They played as HQ and were always known for playing ringers. I think we played in their Wednesday afternoon league for three or four years before they changed things around and Roly, Gary's Dad retired.

Gary's first born was two days earlier than our Daniel and we agreed to do a double head-wetting one midweek evening. Just, Gary, Pete, Brokky and me. The Rat drove his precious SAAB900 from our starting point supping on Hillgate round the corner from the police station and town hall, then tore us up to the Curry Mile in Rusholme for a late meal and then drove us back. Pete drank the same as the rest of us but I suppose as a copper, he would have talked his way out of any interventions by his colleagues. No harm done.

I got a call one night on the direct line we had with Lee Street Police Station, reporting a dead elephant on St. Lesmo Road, which to be fair, did stop me dead in my tracks.

Lots of laughing from the Greater Manchester Police Communicators as they explained that following a number of reports across the country, a gigantic inflatable pink elephant advertising some product in Holland, had blown loose from its moorings and floated across the UK.

I could only imagine the chaos it must have caused the various Air Traffic Controllers up and down the country and planes may well have been diverted. I wasn't to know. All I had to do was galvanise the council resources to clear the road.

Les Cash had become the permanent night highways manager, responsible for delivery of statutory works like road sweeping, gully emptying on the main roads in the quieter hours and responding to emergencies, which were wild and varied. Tonight, it was to cut up and remove a large pink elephant.

Evidently it was spread across the road and hung up around some trees. Les got a cable round it and dragged it all in a mound in the road. Chainsaws chewed up into the plastic, so he resorted to tearing it into big pieces by hooking cables round it and using two lorries pulling in opposite directions before getting JCB's to bucket the big pieces into the backs of the big Foden 8-wheelers hauling big skips. They went into landfill.

He used similar tactics when we got a report of a large articulated lorry from McVities, had gone too fast around Portwood roundabout and shed its load of biscuits. GMP were screaming at us to get the road cleared and all Les could see was the attraction of boxes of biscuits.

The JCB's did their work and he filled several skips before an industrial tow truck appeared to right the McVities lorry and drag it away. The road was open to traffic before the morning peak.

Back at Georges Road Depot, Les arranged for all the undamaged boxes of biscuits to be stacked in a neat pile. Then he and his team used the JCB to push all the broken ones and shit from the crash into a mound around it. I guess he had done something similar in a previous life.

McVities insurance loss adjustor came the following day, saw the pile of shit and condemned the lot. He even agreed to pay a fee for disposal. That night the shit covering was removed and the good boxes of biscuits were carefully extracted and distributed to all and sundry. We got our share of the salvage reward and dined on chocolate digestives and ginger biscuits to dunk in our cuppa's for weeks.

Chapter Eleven

Car Trouble

Finishing the Council Control Room late shift one evening in December, I decided to use the drive home to post some Christmas cards I had written out. I was tired, it was dark, cold and drizzling a bit. I turned onto Chatham Street for the straight run across the back of Edgeley to our house on Northgate Road.

Recently, the council had decided to cut out the rat run of Chatham Street but changing a number of priority's at certain junctions and giving the crossing traffic right of way. As I approached the junction with Bulkeley Street, I noted that it was now a give way for me and slowed down. A car coming across the junction from the opposite direction must have kidded me, as took my foot off the brake and slowly passed him. The BOOM of impact therefore came as a great shock, as a Renault came hurtling down Bulkeley Street at full pelt and our wings collided.

He shot off the road entering the corner shop by its locked door and previously sound large plated window and I was left facing east on Bulkeley Street looking out my bonnet which was wrapped over my windscreen thinking "What the fuck was that?"

Lots of people had heard the crash and came out to investigate and helped by calling the police. I was still sat in my car when the Renault driver climbed out of his car and exited the shop through the open window and the police arrived.

The two coppers split up and one asked me to step out of the car and asked if I had been drinking. No, I had just finished work and was delivering Christmas cards, besides, I hadn't had a drink for over a week as the flu bug had hit me and had been poorly. He still breathalysed me, as standard practice, who knows the lies people will tell when they are detained by the police.

The cop asked me if I had my licence and proof of insurance with me and I said no. He notes I lived not more than half a mile from the scene and said he would accompany me home and check the details there. He commented that this was the fourth accident at this junction since the council changed the priorities and we both noted the illuminated give way sign that wasn't, as it hadn't been connected yet. Typical council. Perhaps the insurance company would be sympathetic.

At that point, the Renault driver was kicking off shouting, just as I was getting into the police car and the cop stopped me. The driver shouted if I was being done. The cop put up his hands in a placating manner and said look, there have been a number of accidents here this last week, it would be for the insurance to sort out and anyway, there were no injuries.

At which point the driver grabbed his elbow and slunk to the floor shouting "Aaaargghhh" and the copper looked at me and said, you make you way home in your own car if it is driveable and I will sort this idiot out and come to see your documents. So, I did.

The copper never came to check my licence or insurance documents, though I sat up and waited for an hour or so and went to bed at midnight musing about what the copper and the Renault driver had got up to.

Insurance sorted things out for the driver as the Renault was declared a write-off. My Third- Party, Fire and Theft policy wasn't going to help my lovely burnt orange (almost red) Ford Cortina MkIII, and I would have to fund the repairs myself.

New off-side wing, new front grill, new bonnet and light cluster fittings. It was clear to me that it wasn't going to be new stuff and so I paid a visit to Royles scrapyard in Portwood.

I spent a day balancing and wrestling with a navy blue MkIII Cortina, piled on top of two other cars in the yard. I managed to retrieve a bonnet, wing, light cluster (but no lamps) and a chrome grille. Whilst the wing could be unbolted on the blue Cortina, that privilege had been denied me on my burnt orange Cortina, as the wing and inner wing were bent to fuck.

Plan B was a visit to see my Uncle Albert, Mum's elder brother. He had welding and cutting gear in his garage, amongst many other tools and furniture stored there. It was a car-less garage, more his workshop than anything else.

I managed to swap out the bonnets but that was the limit of my direct involvement. Uncle Albert got his kit out and put the mask on, then he cut off the old wing, which only took a few moments to be honest. Lots of damp mats on stuff to cover the rubber tyres etc. however, he had less luck when he started to weld on the new (second hand) blue wing. I was stood behind him and saw smoke starting to billow out from the dashboard, inside the car. I began sharply tapping him on his shoulder to catch his attention and stop him as small flames burst out in the engine bay.

Luckily, Uncle Albert was prepared and used a fire extinguisher to put out the flames. We then both surveyed the damage. There was a large black blob where the distributor cap used to be and some of the wiring looked pretty charred. I think we were both amazed that the engine started at the first attempt, so Uncle Albert continued, with more wet mats now in the engine bay and welded on the blue wing.

The rest of the afternoon was spent fitting the light cluster and chrome grille in place using a variety of ingenious methods including a bit of welding, some plastic cable ties and brute force. The end result was a car that looked whole, if not fully colour compliant. That was something that could be remedied in time with some spray paint for sure. I picked up some lamps for the light cluster from Remoco.

It was the following night that Bev and I nicknamed the car Christine. If you haven't seen the movie "Christine" it would be hard to explain. Suffice to say, the car would come alive at frequent and occasionally, unattended times that became a cause for concern.

The first was gone midnight when one of our neighbours from across the road knocked us up to turn off the music in our car…. The radio had turned itself on and was blasting out tunes from Key 103. There was no key in the ignition, though I did check after unlocking the car door. The on/off button on the radio was being overegged by something. So, I toggled it on and off and it stopped.

The neighbour knocked us up again at about 2 in the morning, when the radio turned itself on again, so I disconnected one of the batteries leads.

Driving down the road the following day, the horn decided to shock nearby pedestrians when it came full on, accompanied by the headlights flashing full beam on and off, despite both my hands being on the steering wheel. Hard to explain as you are driving past a group swearing and gesticulating adults and I just carried on.

Standard routine became to disconnect the battery last thing at night, and I decided that we best try to sell it or scrap it.

Unbelievably, a girl and her mechanic brother came to buy it at a give-away £200 as a part repaired, accident damaged car. He said he could sort it out and so I made sure he signed my little note that said "Sold as Seen" as I pocketed the cash. Goodbye Christine.

Having Daniel and Jamie, with Bev expecting and carrying Nicola, we needed another car and our third car was a lovely little Mexico Orange Ford Escort MkII, I picked up for a song.

We were shopping one day in 1990. Pregnant Bev and little Jamie in a trolley. We made our way back to the surface car park on Great Egerton Street behind Toy and Hobby and I realised it had gone. Bev said, "The cars gone, where has the car gone?" and I said it's been stolen "Yes" said Bev, but where has it gone?"

We had left it to the last minute to finish shopping and then go and pick up Daniel from school. I managed to keep calm and sort out the logistics and time in my head. We would never have time to get a cab, even get to the cab rank, and get up to school before he came out with no-one to meet him. So, I asked Bev if she was okay pushing the trolley and hanging the shopping bags off it and walk to the cab rank whilst I ran the two miles to school to pick up Daniel. Bev confirmed it was okay and off I ran.

Born in Stockport - Grew up in the Royal Navy

I did the two miles, with a tough uphill climb out of the town centre, at a good rate. I managed to get to the gates of Alexandra Park Primary School just as the kids were coming out of the doors and Daniel came out to see my red and sweating face and just wanted to show me the drawing he had done and tell me all about his day at school, as we walked slowly the few hundred yards from school to our house none the wiser. Bev, Jamie and the shopping were already waiting for us when we arrived.

We reported the theft to the police, who called us back a few days later. Our biggest concern were the two £50 Britax baby seats that Daniel and Jamie needed as toddlers but they were still buckled into the back of the car which was parked on the public car park at Maine Road, then Man City's ground, with a jam butty police car sat beside it. I thanked the coppers and they drove away.

The thieves however, had ripped out the radio cassette player, taken our collection of home-made tapes, illegally recorded from the Top 40 radio programme on a Sunday evening. Strangely missing as well was the team bucket and sponge. Then I thought maybe they had used the bucket to take away their musical haul and the sponge on top would look innocent enough as they slunk away from the scene of their crime. The bastards. At least I didn't have to hear Abba for a while.

The orange escort took us all over until Nicola was born and then faced with trying to get three baby chairs on the back seat forced me to purchase the only car in my price range that had a 48" flat back seat to take three 16" wide baby chairs. A Ford Cortina MkIV. The one I bought was mainly blue and lots of blue bumps hiding where it was rusting to bits underneath the paint. That one got nicked as well.

Phil Barrington and I were playing pool for the Rat Pit, the genuine nickname of Bents Lane Social Club in Bredbury. We took it in turns to drive, one week it was him, the following week me. Our standard routine was to decide early if it was going to be a drinking night. If so, we would volunteer to play number one and number two in the pecking order, referee for each other to complete our club commitments, then fuck off back to Edgeley and drink in the War Office (Gardeners Arms) or the Alexandra (The Alex), our locals.

Born in Stockport - Grew up in the Royal Navy

We used to play for both the War Office and the Alex but had sort of fallen out with the people who ran or played for the teams and transferred to the Rat Pit, where I played with mates from football, Rod Haslam, Mark Daniels and the Davies brothers, Neil and Gary.

This particular evening, we did the one-two thing and stepped out of the Rat Pit having only had a couple of pints each and determined to get back to the Alex for a few more and I noticed my car had gone, so turned on my heels to walk back into the club, use the wall phone and call the police.

Phil thought I was joking and that somehow I had sneaked out and moved the car and didn't quite believe I hadn't because I was so calm. I just shrugged and said its down to experience, it wasn't the first time I had a car nicked.

We stayed and drank in the Rat Pit and got a lift back to Edgeley from Mark Daniels.

The police called me the following day to report they had found the car. Not an ounce of damage on it. Nothing stolen. Probably got in and started it with a fucking locker key or something. It was on one of the council estates nearby ran out of fuel. I could only ever afford to put a couple of gallons in the tank in those days and it must have needed topping up, so they hadn't got far.

I decided to exchange it and did a deal with Rob Austin, Pete Fords brother-in-law who ran a little repair garage with his dad, buying and selling cars as a side-line. I traded the rust bucket for a red Vauxhall Cavalier MkII. Well, it had been re-sprayed red and evidently started life in the Vauxhall family as a brown one.

It was driving the cavalier from our house to my bezzy oppo Paul Finch (now married to Judy), for a garden party at their house. We used the M60 as a short cut and came off at Bredbury roundabout at Ashton Road and was driving towards the junction at Stockport Road West when a silver Mercedes shot along the wrong side of the road trying to overtake us all and had to pull in quick to avoid a head on collision with approaching traffic and pushed in front of me causing me to brake extremely hard and cause all the kids in the back to shriek. I immediately saw red and jumped out of my car to go remonstrate with the dickhead of a driver.

He must have seen me coming because he jumped out of his car to face me. I started shouting at him that his idiotic driving was a threat to me and my family and I am carrying precious cargo. He responded by saying that I couldn't afford to hit him, which just incensed me more. I grabbed him, folded his arms up, opened his door and bundled him back into his car and shoved the door shut. All the time growling and shouting that I would kill him if he raised his arms to me. I had precious cargo in my car. Then I stormed back to our car and climbed in.

Nicola wanted to know what precious cargo we were carrying and I turned to her and said, you lot. Your mum and you three are my precious cargo. Then I turned to move off as the lights had changed to green. Why isn't he moving off I shouted. To which Daniel said "I'm not sure he can drive from the back-seat Dad…"

I slowly made my way past him and saw his frightened looking face peering at us from the back seat of the Mercedes as other drivers, who had probably not seen the incident, beeped their horns in annoyance. I didn't care, we pressed on to the barbecue.

Chapter Twelve

Keeping fit

When I first came out of the navy, I had palled up with Pete Ford, son of my Dad's mate, and Paul Finch. Being ex-services and like-minded individuals, we had a lot in common. Our wives always got on like a house on fire and we socialised and holidayed a lot together as families.

One evening, late 1981, when we came out of the pub, we had a donkey ride race, with the girls on our backs, we ran down the road, also joined by Phil Barrington and his wife Kate. The four lady riders were hurling good natured abuse at each other and urging on the male donkey's, whilst the four lads were wheezing and completely enveloped in the competition of the race.

Winning was the last thought on my mind as I slipped off the kerb and both Bev and I crunched down onto the road surface. Paul and rider had won, we limped in last. Turned out I had chipped a bone in my ankle and it was agony. Took a while to repair and I didn't play football for ages.

Pete had a long-term lung disease that would eventually end his life before his due term that he had caught whilst serving in the RAF. Some of the advice he received was to stay as fit as he could for as long as he could and he wanted to run a marathon. He tried to persuade me to join him and I said I would run with him to get fit but running a marathon was not on my list of "Must Do's."

We went on a twelve-week no alcohol and carbohydrate fuelling diet and ran most evenings after work and at weekends. I didn't even own a pair of proper running shoes and used to jog with him in my adidas samba football trainers. Unbeknown to me, Pete had completed the entry forms to run in the Stockport Daffodil Marathon, in April 1982, the town's first mass participation event of that decade.

I cannot believe now that I ran that first marathon in a pair of football trainers. It nearly crippled me and my feet were a mess. Pete went out and bought me a pair of blue Hi-Tec road running shoes in sympathy and told me were entered into the Manchester, Piccadilly Marathon the following month and the Bolton Pony Marathon later in the year. Outstanding.

We both ran the Manchester and Bolton Marathons the following year as well. By now I was playing football for Metro FC and I found the injuries not compatible with each other. We continued to run for a few more years, completing half-marathons, 10k races and other distances to raise money for charity and collect the gongs. We had a lot of fun until it came to the point that Pete's breathing got more difficult and he had to give it up.

Whilst I had the bug for running and still do, I stopped attending the events and just used jogging as an infill bit of fitness work to go with my football training.

I was having some problems breathing anyway and regularly suffered from blinding headaches in a morning that were strange considering I was dry most working days of the week.

Reporting my predicament to my GP revealed a simple reason for my headaches, my nose that was broken in 1977 meant that my septum was at a 45-degree angle and mainly blocking both nasal air passages and could be resolved in a simple operation. Right, I thought, let's get on the list. In the end I waited over 3 years.

I kept getting a date for surgery but then it would be cancelled and re-arranged as it was not an emergency and identified as an elective procedure evidently. Anyhow, one day the usual cancellation letter had more to it, with an offer of speeding up the process if I selected local anaesthetic instead of a general. Ring this number if you want to know more. Well, I did and so I called.

The lady who answered was quite patient when I asked what the difference was between a local and a general anaesthetic. She asked me if I was squeamish. I thought, a lad who was a butcher, who served in HM Armed Forces and said, no not me. She started to check dates and I got a little thought that jangled at the back of my mind. Let me just speak to my sister-in-law and I will call you back.

My sister-in-law Christine was a nurse, so I called her and asked her the same question after explaining the purpose of the call. She said that she had worked in surgery for a short while as part of her training and a man had to have his nose broken and re-set with local anaesthetic. She described the tools used by the surgeon. Essentially a big wooden chisel with a rubber end is placed between the nose and cheek bone. Then the surgeon hits the chisel with a big hammer and does the same thing on the other side. The patient is then X-rayed to make sure the bones have broken and the look on that poor man's face as they lay him down for the surgeon to hit him once more was awful.

I decided right at that moment that I was indeed squeamish and called the hospital to reassure them I would wait a bit longer for the opportunity to have a general anaesthetic.

The opportunity finally arose in the summer of 1990. A simple operation, in one day and out the next. I did the wave thing that must bore nurses to death, we all smiled as they put me to sleep and I woke up in hell.

The pain in my head was excruciating and I couldn't see anything as the swelling and wadding I would discover they had stuffed my nasal passages with was blocking my view.

Hey up he's awake announced one of the nurses, who proceeded to pull the curtains round the bed, shove a bowl under my face and tug out the wadding. It came out like a long red and dripping bratwurst that made my eyes tickle as it was pulled out. Followed by a gush of bright red blood.

The nurse dabbed at the mess that over spilled onto my pyjama top, took away the full bowl and put another one under me whilst she took out the second big red sausage. An ice pack on my face helped stop the bleeding and at least I could see again. The headaches were something else and the nurses fed us morphine tablets the first day, reducing them and replacing them with paracetamol the second.

Pete was my only visitor as Bev had her hands full with Daniel, Jamie and the new arrival Nicola. Pete had thoughtfully brought me some things to cheer me up. A porny mag which he shoved under my pillow so I could have a pull later and a can of draft Guinness, which he promptly opened with a hiss and poured into the jug that was for water.

We giggled and shared the Guinness before the nurses got a bit angry with him and shooed him out of the ward. What a lad. I gave the porny mag to one of the nightshift male nurses, as having a wank was the last thing on my mind.

I went home the following day with short cotton plugs up inside the plastic cones the surgeon left up my nose. I had to return some weeks later when he removed them in a not so gentle manner and announced it was successful but I should return in six months and have the other side done. Fuck that. I never went back and have struggled with breathing up one side ever since.

The whole situation wasn't helped when new-born Nicola, at only six weeks of age could shout the house down when she was hungry, did so in the middle of the night two or three nights after I got home.

Bev went downstairs to warm a bottle up and I was cradling a small Tasmanian Devil in my arms when Nicola leaned back and butted me on the nose. That hurt.

I dropped back onto the double bed and rolled Nicola to one side as I tried to hold my nose, stop the blood from cascading over the bedding and hand the Tasmanian Devil over to Beverly. Which I did and retreated to the bathroom in a flood of tears and blood. Cheers Nikki.

Chapter Thirteen

Metrolink (trams in Manchester)

Following a lengthy recruitment and selection process, on the 15th of April 1991 Mo Perkins started work on the trams in Manchester with Greater Manchester Metro Limited (GMML) responsible for operations and maintenance of the trams and the network across Greater Manchester.

Born in Stockport - Grew up in the Royal Navy

Initially employed as a Senior Controller, I was responsible for the safe and efficient delivery of tram services whilst on duty. A senior supervisor, junior manage role working shifts 24/7. I was part of the initial intake into what is now a world-famous tram system. However, the early days were fraught with challenges....

This would be the beginning of the smoothing out of my scallywag approach to life as I got my first proper civilian supervisory / management position as a Senior Controller. We would write the rule book and training manuals for Controllers and Light Rail Vehicle (LRV) Drivers as they were first called. Tram drivers these days I guess.

In the first few months of recruitment, I was part of a group of 10 of the new employees who were sent over to Brussels to learn to drive trams and get a better understanding of the challenges of street running (Metrolink was the first light rail / tram system to run in traffic since trams were withdrawn in the 1950s and 60's). we were to provide the cadre of training all the new staff needed to operate and maintain Metrolink in Manchester.

Evening socialising and team building was a common theme throughout the 5 weeks or so we were there. On one such evening, there as a scramble to get into the small lift in the apartment block we were billeted in. 5 of the guys (Mark Terry, Ray Catterall, Dave Maxwell, Tony Cavanagh and Alan Higgins) jumped into a lift meant for 3 people. As the doors closed one of them stuck 2 fingers out at the rest of us who now had to climb the stairs. But as we took the first steps, there was a loud thump as the lift ground to a halt….

Those of us walking fell about laughing and we going to leave them to their plight. I distinctly remember Mick Brown saying "Fuck em, they pushed us out of the way and locked the main entrance door so we couldn't get in". Our plan was then to return to our apartments but one was shouting that he was claustrophobic, so I thought I had better go and get help.

There was a sign next to the lift door "Depannage" and a telephone number. Mo ran down the street to a hotel and asked the concierge if he could use the hotel phone as some of his friends were stuck in the lift. What follows is what I recall from the rendition of the phone call:

Mo: "Parlez vous English"

Lift company: "Non"

Mo: "Is this the Depannage lift company?"

Lift company: "Depannage?"

Mo: "Yes, Depannage"

Lift company: "Depannage?"

Mo: raised voice "Are you the Depannage Lift Company?"

Lift company: "Cest leDepannage?"

Mo: Yes, the Depannage !!

At which point, the concierge said "Please let me" as he took the phone and spoke in rapid French to the lift company. He then said "This is the Schindler lift company. They want to know what your emergency (depannage) is….

Mo: short pause whilst he regained some composure and said "The lift in our apartment block has broken down with some of my colleagues in it"

Concierge: rapid exchange of French, then "Schindler will send out a repair man as soon as possible"

I thanked him very much for his help and ran back to the apartment block. Told the lads in the lift that someone was coming and buggered off to bed. It would not be the first breakdown in translation whilst we were working there.

That wasn't the end of the lift story of course. Mark Terry (now VP of Mott MacDonald light rail engineering worldwide), had a small screwdriver set in his jacket........ like you do on a night out and had proceeded to undo the lift control panel cover and was fiddling with the electrics. This didn't go down too well with the Schindler lift repair man who arrived about an hour later.

The company received an invoice for around £800 from Schindler for repairs caused by overcrowding and tampering with the lift panel.... Allegations that were strenuously denied. Not sure if the bill was paid or not...

Me and Mick were being trained by Josef van de Loo, who liked to be known as Jef. His English wasn't great but certainly far better than our pidgin French and non-existent Walloon. However, we got by most days.

Jef took us on the street running sections, the pre-metro (underground) tram sections, showed us how to change points, how to round a roundabout in circles whist he got his breakfast and had us stopped in all manner of sidings and termini as he indulged in his favourite pastime of smoking and testing his English out on us. A lovely guy, with a good sense of humour. However, his attempt at humour almost caused an accident.

We had taken the Brussels "Rules and Regulations" course, to learn all the signs, the highway code aspect of driving on the street and numerous other formal requirements before we were let out on the network. A tram stop sign is a big red circle on a white background for instance.

One day, we were hurtling down the light rail section near to Anderlecht stadium and it was my turn to drive, with Jef stood close by and Mick in the seat immediately behind. Watching each other drive was as much a learning curve as driving yourself, a good process mimicked today by most UK tram operators. As we approached a tram stop, the following exchange took place...

Jef: "Mo, watch out for the Chinese flag."

Mo: peering intently into the distance can see a heavy rail crossing sign (basically a big red X) and a warning sign for some points ahead but is struggling to make sense of Jef.

Jef: a little agitated "Mo, watch out for the Chinese flag."

Mo: properly squinting into the distance and cannot see anything resembling a Chinese flag.

Jef: now very agitated and jumping up and down at the side of Mo pointing to the tram stop.

Mo: jams the brakes on and skids into the tram stop shouting "It's a Japanese flag, you wanker!"

As we shudder to a halt, Jef says questioningly "Chinese flag?"

Mo: "No, a Chinese flag is a red flag with golden stars on it, the Japanese flag is a big red circle on a white background!!"

Jef: holding his hand to his mouth and looking shocked "Oh, mon dieu, of course" ......

At the end of the driving course, our group wanted to take out all the instructors and their partners for a meal and present them with a gift. We all took an action, presents for the guys, presents for the girls, book the restaurant, gather the cash off all the Brits, etc. Mine was a bunch of flowers for each of the ladies. Easy peasy, I thought and went straight off to the florists down the street.

Mo: "Parlez vous Anglais?"

Florist: "Non"

Mo: "Okay then, I need some flowers"

Florist: "Fleur?"

Mo: "Yes, Fleur. A bunch of them"

Florist: "A baunch?" she looks at her colleague and both give a gallic shrug

Mo: "Yes, a bunch, a gathering of flowers together, sort of wrapped up a bit, sometimes tied up with a ribbon and bow"

Florist: states helpfully "a bouquet?"

Mo: blushing (of course), "Yes, a bouquet" counts fingers and says "Sept bouquet, s'il vous plait"

Florist: "Oui" and gets to work

Mo: hopes the world will open up so I can step into the hole, whilst the florists make up 7 bouquets. For fuck sake.

I still retain the certificate, presented to us all in a lovely ceremony, qualifying me to drive trams in Brussels.

When we got back to the UK, we all took the lead in something, mine was radio operations and the control room as I was the only senior recruit with experience of working in a control room.

The layout of the original Metrolink Control Room was famously and unkindly referred to as resembling a Tandy Workshop (cheap electrical wholesaler and retailer of the 90's). Created and set up by a project engineering team from GEC Alstom, it had clearly not been constructed with any regard to the natural flow of communications that control room operations create. With separate systems placed far apart across a single desk facing a bank of signalling monitors and CCTV screens.

As the operations team lead for the control room, I was invited into one of the project meetings to "sign off" the control room ready for operations. A meeting full of tension as the engineers wanted to fuck off to their next project as quickly as possible and Greater Manchester Metro Limited (GMML) the Operations & Maintenance company, unwilling to give up warranty's, wanted the system to be fully tested and challenged during the "work up" phase of running trams to a timetable without passengers before they did fuck off.

I was quietly fuming at the inability of the operations senior management to convey the reality of what is expected to be handed over but isn't. My agitation began to come to the attention of the GEC Project Director Jeff Done, who was sat next to me.

Just as I was about to be invited to speak and had taken a deep breath ready to vent to all and sundry, Jeff leaned over me quite deliberately and reached for the coffee pot. Whilst he did, he whispered "Think about your career path son" which really deflated me but did give me a moment to recover and I did use his wise advice.

I articulated the challenge of spreading the systems to far across the control desk and with only one or two operators using the kit would be inefficiency personified, as they moved from side to side every minute or so to do their job. Jeff Done asked me what I would do? I then proceeded to use pieces of notepaper to indicate systems and places them in a more sensible and ergonomic manner, arranging them across the meeting room table. I outlined my reasoning and a rough estimate of call volumes and types. My logic was received well, whether they really understood or not.

The outcome was, some of systems had to have duplicate screens and keyboards installed, in order to provide the operators with the access to what they needed, without constantly moving across seven or eight foot of desk to do each task.

One thing I didn't forget, was that advice from Jeff Done, those wise words were really to take a deep breath and make your argument with logic and reasoning, not anger and recrimination. My first lesson in don't get upset by what happened, be judged on what you do about it.

One of the reasons that Metrolink had recruited me, was to take a lead on all thing's radios. I had to get to grips with how the system operated in a technical way and then create an appropriate set of radio procedures that could be trained to all Metrolink staff. It was a partially trunked private mobile radio network, for those who need the techy stuff.

The initial radio system operated on 2 frequencies. One was a data channel and one was audio. The system required the tram and the control room to technically "handshake" and then a unique audio call could be undertaken between the controller and tram driver. It was only at the successful conclusion of the handshake (exchange of data between tram and control system) that any audio could commence.

In the event of a system failure, the fall back was to a single audio channel, open to all. I had to devise a set of radio protocols that would incorporate the handshake and also be used in an open channel situation. It was simple and quite clever. The radio procedures are still in place today, 25 years on and counting....

For the radio training, we used to have one instructor in the cab of a parked tram in the depot and one in the control room, so as not to interfere with normal and day to day operations. It enabled us to use all the different emergency procedures that were drilled into all staff, in a controlled environment. All operational and engineering staff had been programmed onto the courses, as staff mobile on the system also carried hand portable radios (mobile telephones were in their infancy in the early 90's).

One such the day, the Engineering Director, Jim Harries came into the control room and was observing the training. He had previously expressed a concern that his staff needed to attend the 1-day course and the Operations Director had clearly pointed him in the direction of Mo. So, in he came when he saw me in the Control Room.

Jim interrupted the training in a loud voice (probably to make sure that everyone in the control room could see him exercising his status) "Excuse me Mo, please can you tell me why I and my engineers, most of whom are already HNC or ONC trained, need to attend this 1-day radio course."

Everyone in the room looks at me. I turned to Jim and handed him a radio. "Okay Jim, please call Tommo on the radio?"

"Certainly," says Jim "Which button do I press?"

"Exactly!" I announced, "and the reason why you and your engineers need to attend the 1-day radio course" and grabbed the radio back.

Jim, silenced, stomps out of the control room to much mirth and laughter. However, I knew he would be off whingeing to the Operations Director and I would get my just rewards in due course, no doubt. And I did.

Scott Helliwell was the OD then and whilst he thought it was hilarious and took Jim down a peg and he agreed with the requirement for everyone to attend the course to get consistency, he had struggled against Jim's argument on his competent engineers. My stance was the right thing.

However, he also needed to bollock me to support the management view. So, he did.

It was a quiet bollocking and no report on my personal file. Cheers Scott.

The core team that began the company that GMML would become, set out a number of key principles for the organisation. No-one had operated trams in the UK, other than the heritage system at Blackpool and new rules, applicable to fast light rail (50mph) on segregated lines, alongside "line-of-sight" tram operations in the heavily trafficked and pedestrianised city centre of Manchester.

GMML could not just recruit tram drivers, they didn't really exist at that time and so erred on people who could think on their feet and would not be burdened by any perceived demarcation lines that may be set by others. In doing so, they innocently targeted people like me. Guys and girls that had served in HM Armed Forces and people who think like we do. The result was the organisation was made up of about 35% of ex-services staff.

GMML wanted everyone to be staff, regardless of role. Quite forward thinking in those far-off days. We would all be salaried and paid directly into bank accounts. No-one was considered to be an hourly rated role.

Those early years were all about making mistakes, learning from them and getting better. We all mucked in to help each other and it created a camaraderie that only those with HM Armed Forces experience, could identify with. We socialised together at both company events and private parties, along with pub crawls and birthday runs. Some of which were not for the faint hearted.

When Sheffield wanted to construct its own tram network, called Supertram, the client and operator reached out and recruited a number of Metrolink personnel. We held joint incident planning sessions to share knowledge and good practice. This over spilt into our annual football match and social event. The first of which was Metrolink heading over the Pennines to be hosted by Supertram.

Somewhere along the line, there must have been a mix up in communications. The Metrolink Social Club hired a coach and around 50+

staff, accompanied by loads of crates of beer and wine, set off on the journey to meet a slightly larger and family oriented Supertram outfit, complete with partners and children. We were both a little shocked to realise that we when we met up on sunny but very windy day, as drunken people spilled out of the coach clutching bottles of booze.

Supertram had hired a sports ground, with a lovely pitch and a bar. Even playing drunk, the guys won 3-1 in an eleven a side game and the girls won a five a-side match. Then we went onto to party until it got dark and the coach driver warned he was running out of hours.

We did manage to get everyone back on the coach, many worse for wear for a drunken singalong back to Manchester. Sean Dutton and John McGhee forced open the fresh air skylight at the back of the coach, climbed out onto the roof and "surfed" all the way down Woodhead, a particular winding and dangerous piece of road over the Pennines and the most direct route back to town. I think we lost some or all of our deposit to pay for the skylight repair.

The event was repeated again the following four years and we made more effort for it to be a family balanced affair. The Metrolink guys won every year and the girls, now playing eleven a side as well, weighed in with one win and two draws before the annual event was cancelled after Supertram hit a number of financial blockers.

Despite best attempts, over the next few years, I managed to stay out of trouble or not get caught, which is a fine balance between planning and downright luck and in February 1996 I was promoted to Traffic Manager. I made an immediate impact and all was looking good as we approached the contract re-bid, where I added value into the GEC-led bid team. Moving onto working days after shifts since I was seventeen years old was a shock but it came with the bonus of weekends off and all nights in.

Unfortunately, an incident occurred that resulted in my arrest and court appearance which needed to be disclosed to the company, under the terms and conditions of my employment.

Daniel had been playing football for a junior club run by one of my cousins with whom I was not related, not confusing at all. He enjoyed it but I had told him I didn't want to get involved in any more management and certainly not junior football as too many parents seem to think that their Johnny or Billy is going to be the next Wayne Rooney. Really.

As it was, I got sucked in. A bit of help coaching here, referee that game there. Oh, the manager is ill, will you help us out on match day. Things like that and was appointed as Assistant Manager. I helped run a club fund raising event by booking out a local recreation centre and swimming pool just for club families. We had inflatables in the pool, table tennis, badminton and other stuff on in the hall, culminating in some 5 a-side for the kids and then a fateful Dads v Dads game that got a bit out of hand.

The club chairman, a lad similar age to me who fancied himself as a footballer but he clearly wasn't, "boarded me" and ran me into the wall. I just laughed and the next time he got the ball I fouled him. We did a couple of tit for tat trips before he confronted me. I just laughed it off and said kick me and I'll kick you back.

What didn't help was the high number of spectators who witnessed it from the glassed off viewing area in the bar. They could see what happened but couldn't hear. I was somehow painted as the aggressor but I was just standing up for myself. It wasn't going to help matters later on.

The following Wednesday I was taking training for the under 11's who Daniel played for, as the Manager had broken his ankle. The boys had done a bit of fitness work and we were ending the session with a match and I was doing my coaching.

One of the lads won a good tackle, stood up and hoofed the ball up the pitch and as I ran beside him I asked him to look up next time he won the ball, as he had space to work with. Try and keep a picture of everything around you, don't just clog the ball hopefully, look and make a proper pass. He nodded that he understood and I turned round to find that the ball was out of play and the boys were arguing over who's throw in it was.

I jogged over and asked the boys to be sensible, you know who's throw it is, it is just a training session. If you cannot agree, then I will do a drop ball. One of the boys said it was the opponents throw as he had kicked it out. As I thanked him and say we can now get on with the game, the chairman's youngest son who was our goalkeeper shouted out "I told you it was our throw you fucking wanke.r"

It caught me by surprise but I blew my whistle to remonstrate with him about swearing at a coach. As I did so, I could see his dad, the chairman motoring onto the pitch running straight for me shouting at me. I turned round to see him throwing a punch but I just ducked and stepped up into him. I did think about dropping him there and then but didn't. He tried to throw a second punch but I dodged him again. I could have hit him as he was wide open but I didn't. At that point, the chasing pack of parents pulled us both apart and we called an end to training. I had not raised my hands at all. He was arguing that I had pointed at his son and wouldn't hear anything about the swearing. I wasn't to speak to his son.

A few days later my cousin called me to say that I needed to resign. I hadn't wanted to be appointed as Assistant Manager in the first place but couldn't see what I had done wrong and refused to resign. He said that he had no other choice but to sack me for my indiscretions ongoing feud with the chairman. WTF. I could continue watching the games but would not be able to coach. Evidently the chairman kept his job. It angered me immensely that I had been treated the way I had.

So, there we are on a Saturday morning on the windswept slopes of a crappy little pitch in Whaley Bridge. We play downhill in the first half, with the gale-force wind behind us and are winning 2-0 at half time against a particularly good team.

The manager told the players to keep the ball on the ground as much as possible in the second half, with the keeper rolling the ball out to either full back or central defenders when he could.

Whaley Bridge score two quick goals in the first few minutes of the second half and after yet another attack in our half had broken down the keeper kicked the ball out of his hands. It went up in the air and looped back over the defenders into the gap between them and the now stranded keeper. Their forward, clearly reading the wind better than our players ran onto it and thumped it into the back of the net to go 3-2 up.

The goalkeeper then shouts at my son Daniel the left fullback that it's all his fault. I along with several other players told him to be quiet and it was his poor choice of kick that had caused the goal.

His father was already hurtling down the touchline towards me shouting that he told me to never speak to his son again and at which point I had reached my limit. I told him in simple words, including a number of expletives to stay where he was and not to come anywhere near me, otherwise I would flatten him.

He carried on towards me calling me a tough guy and I replied that I am so tough, I'm going to let you have the first swing as I handed my spectacles to Beverly stood beside me and he launched himself at me.

As he swung, I felt my arms being pressed to my sides as his mate, an off-duty copper clamped my arms and it took all my effort to pull my head back and so only get a glancing blow to the face. Bev ran in between us and the chairman threw her to the floor. My good mate Jimmy Kearney jumped on the copper and gave him a dig, that freed me up and I jumped on the chairman and battered him. I lost count of the punches I hit him with.

As everyone piled in to break us up, someone caught my punching arm in a hold and I couldn't reach his face. He had fallen down into a kneeling position, face down but my left hand was free, so I grabbed his face with it and started pulling his mouth and nose up. He squealed and pulled upwards away from my hand, allowing me to get a few more punches in before we got separated.

His face was a mess with lots of blood streaming from his nose, his mouth and round his eyes. I had hardly a mark on me.

The game was abandoned by a horrified and bemused opposition and we went our various ways. We went home but the copper and the chairman went to the local police station to file an assault charge and then onto A&E. A few days later I was invited into Chapel en le frith police station.

Following some advice from my real cousin Barbara's detective husband, I employed a brief and he accompanied me there, where I was arrested on assault and causing an affray and had all the fingerprint and DNA stuff taken. The police refused to hear my side of the story and I was informed to make another appointment on another day to do that. They were just being awkward.

As the brief and I left the police station, two of the coppers followed me down the corridor reeling off my previous civilian court offences, going all the way back to my under-age motor bike charges in 1974, the D&D in Pompey, Drunk and Theft of beer mugs in Brighton. I said to the brief that they can't do that can they, statute of limitations or something was supposed to clear your record after ten years. He just told me to keep on walking and not to respond, which is what they wanted. So, we did.

It took some time for the Derbyshire police to host me and Beverly, so that we could give our version of the events. That I had warned him not to approach, that he had threw the first punch and that he had thrown Beverly to the floor. It took a long time for the statement to be taken. Eventually it was.

I believe that we were both charged with the same offences and due to appear in Buxton magistrates court, though on different dates.

My brief was absolutely amazing and got me off everything as long as I agreed to be bound over to the keep the peace for twelve months. Which I did. He even got all our costs paid for by the court. Well done. He said that his firm would not make anything out of the case and would I consider donating to the practice. I suggested £50 and was happy with that. So was I.

I don't know how the chairman fared but the truth was, he hit me first and threw Bev to the floor. As far as I was concerned, he deserved everything he got. If it ever happened again, I would hit him even harder.

The Operations Director was pretty dubious about the whole thing from the moment I told him I had been charged, I assume he thought I would be found guilty and kept me at arms-length for a few months, probably in case he had to sack me. Who knows? He changed his opinion of me that is for sure. We still keep in touch via professional circles and get on very well. I should have put a sign on my office door, for people to beware that this dog bites. Ha ha.

In 1997 GMML lost the operations and maintenance contract for Metrolink to ALTRAM. A consortium of Ansaldo Trasporti, John Laing PLC and Serco. All the O&M staff "TUPE'd" to Serco a large company who didn't seem to specialise in transport but delivered lots of central government services in the newly privatised public sector. Ansaldo would provide new trams and upgrade all the systems, whilst Laings would construct the new extension to Eccles.

The Transfer of Undertakings (TUPE) legislation was supposed to guarantee that everyone kept their job as we moved from one company to another. It does for the most but quite often, the incoming provider will have made financial calculations based on becoming more efficient and saving money. Sometimes this is through restructuring the organisation and losing roles, which formed a key part of the Altram solution, that along with drastically changing the timetable. It didn't work.

Without going into lots of boring technical details. The timetable change was a non-starter and didn't generate savings or increased revenue. Therefore, no redundancies and we pretty much carried on as before, except the Private Finance Initiative (PFI) model had insufficient income to pay off its debts. A miscalculation on the rate of inflation put the final nail in the coffin and ALTRAM went non-financial in the year of the Commonwealth Games held in Manchester in 2002.

I was promoted to Assistant Operations Director and reported into a new board at Metrolink. The new OD was called away to intervene in another contract and I became acting OD for the next 9 months whilst the organisation wrestled with the new challenges and a complete restructure of the business.

The MD was outed over his miscalculations, poor relationship with the client and our Engineering Director took over as MD. He also started the search for a new OD and I hoped that all my good work would stand in me in good stead. However, it didn't.

I found out when he called me into his office and told me a new guy was joining us from Docklands Light Railway. He said he knew I was disappointed, but it wasn't my time. He went on to say that our divisional MD was coming up today and will be offering me a temporary role out in Australia.

I thought "Fuck, they don't want me for the job I have been doing so well for the last 9 months and are now transferring me to a penal colony, could it get any worse!"

Chapter Fourteen

Australian Adventure

In May 1998, I went out to Melbourne for a week. It arose when the Divisional MD explained that our Asia Pacific colleagues were going to be bidding for the up-and-coming privatisation of the tram and train network in Melbourne being tendered by the Victoria State Treasury Department. Wow.

I would need to go there for a week in May and about three months in September. I explained that I needed to discuss this with Beverly. I think, he thought that I was negotiating and said that if it were a day over three months, the whole family could go. Wow. I really did need to talk this over with Bev, it was a major intervention into all what we were doing. So, I went home for a chat.

Bev said "No."

She was not going to go to Australia. She had millions of questions and I had very few answers. She proper dug her feet in and said we were not going to go.

I had to secure a business visa myself, strange that the company didn't do it for me, it had to be an individual application but endorsed by Serco. It only got sorted about a week before I flew out. Bev came to say goodbye at the airport but we were barely on speaking terms and it wasn't a pleasant farewell at all.

I had never flown Business Class before and in fact, had made very few plane journey's in my life. This was probably the second in total honesty. The only other time I flew, was on a Thomson's package holiday to Majorca in 1982 when Bev and I finally celebrated our honeymoon. Two years after getting married. We just never had any money. We had even less after the children were born.

At the Manchester airport check in desk, the staff advised me that my luggage would be patched right through to Melbourne and to enjoy the flight. The transfer at Heathrow was seamless and I jumped on a bus to take me from one terminal to another.

We arrived on the Sunday and we had a lazy day taking in some of the sights, a bite to eat and a few drinks.

Monday commenced, with a whirlwind of activity as I met some of the other colleagues I would be working with and we had a number of organised visits and meetings arranged by the Treasury Department. We met with the management teams of both tram companies and both train companies, saw some of the depot's and met with key supply chain partners, legal and financial organisations.

In the middle of the week, we had a sojourn with one of the big finance houses who would partner with us at a retreat out on the Mornington Peninsula, which included subject areas I had not got a clue about. Things like cross border currency exchanges, net present values and return on equities that had me concerned about what I had let myself in for.

However, it was when one of the finance guys started talking about tram operations and was literally speaking bollocks that I raised my hand and said something like, no mate, that's not how it works at all. I then rambled on for a few minutes explaining how it really worked. I just saw a room full of smiling faces and suddenly I realised why I was there. I may not have understood the financial stuff at that time but I definitely knew how to deliver safe and efficient tram operations and what's more, I knew a damn sight more than anyone else in the room.

After five days of meetings, eating buffets, drinking until very late. Some of the Aussies wanted to demonstrate their prowess over the Poms, which they did with most but not with me. We split up and I got another flight home on the Saturday morning.

A lot of the guys had arranged a two-day stopover in Singapore to meet with the people we were going to bid the train contracts with. Singapore Mass Rapid Transport. However, no-one had included me, so mine was straight back to London Heathrow and a hop back up to Manchester.

The Melbourne to Singapore leg was delayed. Something to do with a fault light showing. We were all strapped into our seats and the delay was twenty minutes, then another twenty minutes and we continued that way for two hours. Credit to the cabin crew, who fluttered around dispensing lots of champagne, vino and ale to those in the Business Class section and it generated a bit of a party atmosphere.

It seemed that because of the delay, then the flight time to Singapore, they would get their version of a stand down and a night in Singers. No wonder they wanted to party. Unlike the standby crew we picked up in Singapore. Talk about a game of two halves.

We had to get off the plane whilst it re-fuelled. Some health and safety requirement evidently and I sat outside in the transfer lounge for an hour or so trying to sober up. When we were allowed back on board the plane I was disappointed to find that the humid air outside had conflicted with the air conditioning inside the plane and big drips from the condensation had pooled on my seat.

I approached the cabin crew to request a seat change or at the very least, something waterproof to sit between my bum and the wet seat. I was quite shocked by the response I got from one of the crew who just told me to sit down. When I tried to protest that the seat was wet, he challenged me that I had been drinking and if I were drunk and causing problems, he would get me thrown off the plane!

So, I went back to my seat. It is true that I had been drinking, all the free booze dished out by the party crew on the way there and I had no desire to be dumped in Singapore. Therefore, I took the plastic covered courtesy pillow and shoved it on the seat, then I sat on it and put on my seatbelt.

The lady in the next seat to mine couldn't believe the exchange I had with Mr Disgruntled cabin crew and said I must complain in writing. She gave me her name and said she would be a witness. Once in the air, another member of the cabin crew came over and it was my fellow passenger who explained the circumstances. I then showed her the seat. She confirmed that there were no spare seats unfortunately but provided another blanket and a better piece of polythene to cover the wet seat. I in turn asked her to record the incident in the flight log, which she did.

Mr Disgruntled cabin crew tried to apologise to me later in the flight but I just waved him away without speaking to him. Business Class hand signals evidently carry some weight. When I got home I did indeed write a two-page letter of complaint and sent it to the Chief Executive of Qantas.

The two-hour delay at Heathrow meant I missed the shuttle to Manchester and sat in one of the bars chewing some pints of Stella Artois. About four in all, before boarding the shuttle flight to Manchester.

The jetlag kicked in the following day.

As the frequent flyer I eventually became, I now know that drinking copious amounts of alcohol and minimal amounts of H20 has a massive impact on dehydration, the very foundation of jetlag. Something I strive to avoid and have done so very well ever since then.

It was a week or two before the jetlag finally waned away and I could re-join society properly. It was also a nice surprise when I received a lovely letter from the head of customer services at Qantas containing profuse apologies and information pertaining to the disciplinary action taken against Mr Disgruntled cabin crew. Furthermore, Qantas would be pleased if I would receive two crates of wine (one red and one white) by way of apology, which I did, very gladly.

As we got through the summer of 1998 the idea of spending some time in Australia as a family would be an opportunity that we did not want to pass us by. Bev and I formulated a bit of a plan, with some funny and interesting outcomes but we didn't really receive confirmation until four weeks before we were due to fly out. Then it was all stations go.

We arranged for my cousin Barbara and her beautiful daughter Georgia to take on our house. She was getting divorced from her abusive husband and had been cramped into her Mum Dot's, little terraced house. She just paid for the utilities.

I sold our blue cavalier, we had traded up from the red, nee brown one, to a new model, to my mate Neil Jackson for a £1 on the understanding that he sold it back to me when we got back home. It gave Neil and Mel an extra car for a while.

We banked with Yorkshire Bank. I had got fed up with Barclays charging me interest and fees on holding my money in their bank and transferred to Yorkshire, who were the first bank to offer no fee accounting if you stayed in the black. Good people. We are still with them. I noted that the bank had been set up by the then big four banks, to try out different methods without diluting their own value but they had all sold their interests to National Australia Bank in 1990.

I thought great, I would open an Australian account via the Yorkshire Bank, as I was going to still be paid in the UK and needed to transfer funds to live off, when we were in Australia.

The cashier in Yorkshire Bank told me no. I would have to open an account when we got to Australia, but I couldn't see how I could then arrange for bank transfers from my bank, if I was off down south in the Antipodes. I asked to see the Bank Manager and was told that I needed an appointment. I said she isn't busy, as I could see over the cashier's head and the bank manager was stood in her office watering a plant but the cashier refused. So, I raised my voice a little, as is my want and demanded to see the bank manager as I had a complaint to make about poor customer service to a loyal customer.

It had the desired outcome as Tracey McKee, as I would soon to find out, the recently promoted bank manager, was only too keen to help. She listened patiently to our story about the short notice, cousin living in the house stuff and said she had no idea how she would do it but yes, I was right, NAB were the owners and it stood to reason they would be more than happy to facilitate opening us an account. I gave her the address of the house that Serco leased for us for the bid and she said she would set up an account in the nearest bank and she did.

Bev and the kids would have to travel on a tourist visa. Serco's advice blew very close to the wind, that once they arrive, we would declare that I will be working in Australia and the kids would stay and go to school. Of course, we could not tell the kids that. Daniel aged 13, Jamie aged 10 and Nicola aged 8, all thought we were going on holiday for a few weeks. The same story we told to Alexandra Park Primary School and Avondale High School. That would also be our cover in case anyone asked any intelligent questions at passport control. However, we had to get the flights.

Born in Stockport - Grew up in the Royal Navy

Our children had never flown before and Beverly only once, on our 1982 delayed honeymoon. So, the flight alone was an adventure. What may have appeared as a cost saving to Serco turned into a mini drama for the Perkins family. The rail admin team booked the flights separately. A cheap hop standard to Heathrow, then Business Class with Malaysia Airlines from Heathrow to Melbourne, via Kuala Lumpur.

The check in staff at Manchester airport were a little perplexed that we had two different sets of flight tickets and I can only assume did their best with what they had and off went our luggage.

The British Airways hop to Heathrow entertained a large number of passengers around us as Nicola made whooping noises of joy and excitement from the moment the plane took off down the runway and she felt that thrust, until we landed in Heathrow about 25 minutes later. So, it was all smiles as we filed off and I remembered the route to the transfer shuttle and led our little band, all carrying flight bags to the bus terminal.

Security refused us entry to the transfer shuttle as we did not have through tickets. Thank you Serco. We would have to make our way under the runways on a half-mile long tunnel but first had to walk through the arrival terminal to find it, walk its length, then find our way through the departure tunnel. Outstanding.

The team started to complain early in the walk through the tunnel. Beverly had Nicola on her back in a donkey ride and I held all five flight bags on the sweaty slog through it whilst constantly checking the eroding transfer time. By the time we got to the departure hall most of the lights were out, apart from the Malaysia Airlines desk and we only had about twenty minutes before the plane took off.

We hurried along and a voice boomed out in the darkness. Are you the Perkins family? Yes, we are, I think the whole team cried in unison, with Bev and me hurrying the kids along. It's alright, slow down, you haven't missed the flight, take it easy.

The Malaysia Airlines staff started to check us in and asked why our hold baggage had only been ticketed as far as Kuala Lumpur but of course, we didn't know. They said no worries that they would sort it out. One of their team came onto the plane to speak with me personally to confirm that our baggage was now ticketed all the way to Melbourne and gave me a card with his name and number on it if there were any problems. He also told us to make sure we enjoyed the Lion Club, the Business Class lounge in Kuala Lumpur as we had a couple of hours to kill on the transfer.

Our children have always been polite and tried always to use please and thank you. This went down a storm with the cabin crew on the flight and they fussed around our kids something awful.

Daniel didn't enjoy the flight out and several times said he thought he was going to be sick. I tried to reassure him that he wouldn't be sick and we would be landing soon. It got worse for him as we descended and I thought it would be great as we finally braked to a stop. Then Daniel threw up all over the back of the seat in front of him. Cue lots of fussing around from the lovely cabin crew and lots of apologies from Daniel.

It wasn't until we landed at Kuala Lumpur and began to disembark that Daniel spotted an athlete, I think it was one of the sprinters and then I noticed some of the field athletes that we realised a large contingent of English, Welsh and Scottish athletes were onboard attending the Commonwealth Games in Kuala Lumpur. We had not noticed them as they were back in cattle class, whilst we mere mortals were slumming it in Business Class. They were held back as we exited the plane, quite a surreal thing really. It was the weekend before the opening ceremony, 11th September 1998.

Malaysia Airlines were one of the Games sponsors and they handed a little package to each passenger in Business Class that included a metal coaster, commemorating the games. We had one each and picked up a few more as other Business Class passengers just left them there. You can take the kids out of Stockport but you can't take Stockport out of the kids, as they gleefully scooped up several each. Free stuff, not stealing. We still have the coasters now, all these years later.

Business Class really spoiled my children. A few years later we could afford to go to Florida and experience all that Walt Disney and Universal had to offer in a fun-filled three-week holiday, they all complained on how cramped it was in standard class..... haha and no freebies....

Born in Stockport - Grew up in the Royal Navy

Our Australian Adventure brought the five us together far more closely than we were at home. I didn't have football, the kids didn't have their clubs, so we did lots together once we got over the initial tears.

After we successfully navigated passport control and we got to the house in the eastern suburb of Blackburn, Bev and I sat the kids down and told them the truth. We were going to be here a while. Cue lots of tears and tantrums that lasted the rest of the day.

Things chirped up a lot when we went on a tour of school appointments that my very clever and dry humoured Australian Serco host Lawrence G Norton set up for us.

The first two primary schools we visited didn't impress us or the two little ones that much but it was when we got to Laburnum Primary School that we realised how differently the Aussies do things. We sat down in the Headmasters office after he had taken us round the school and showed us the classrooms and other facilities. I started to ask a question and the head held his hand up said, it should be the children interviewing him, not the parents. It did gob smack me for a moment and then I got my first glimpse of understanding.

Jamie and Nicola patiently asked some questions about all sorts of things, that he and a teacher responded to. They had already made their decision, long before we got into the car that this was the school for them. The teachers had taken a personal interest in the children, something they would go on to do well.

Daniel took one look at Boxhill High School and decided that would be his choice and we cancelled all the other appointments we had. I then went to work, not three days after we landed. The kids were all going to school. The only fly in the ointment was Bev couldn't get a job. Seemed okay at first but it slowly drove her mad.

It took many weeks before Bev got her head around things. Devoid of sensible conversation as she had no friends there, she threw herself into keep fit. She went to the gym and the swimming pool every day and got into a great routine. But it wasn't easy for her.

Born in Stockport - Grew up in the Royal Navy

I wanted to train and play a bit of football and made contact with Melbourne United but the season had just ended. After a lengthy break I was invited to join them for training. I hadn't realised that this was Melbourne United of Australian Pools fame. Now in the lower divisions but a good outfit. We trained two evenings a week and I played in two or three pre-season games before the bid work got too much and I had to give it up. If you didn't train, you were not included in team selection.

Working on a bid creates lots of challenges trying to balance work and home life. This was different because we had no circle of friends outside of work, so that's who we socialised with.

Metrolink back in Manchester was pretty low on technology. I didn't realise that until I landed in Australia and was issued with a laptop computer and a mobile telephone as standard issue. I also had my first encounter with the internet there.

First day in work I met the two colleagues that I would work the closest with, other than Lawrence. Warren (Wazza) Peart and Shane Kirtland, two very experienced and funny guys who liked a beer. We had to pull a presentation together for a team meeting the following day and I said we should put some images of trams in there.

I just typed tram images in the search bar and up popped a load of pornographic links to dodgy websites under tram image, tramp image, fuck horny wives thing….. I did think for fuck sake as I tried desperately to delete the filth that popped up. My colleagues just fell about laughing. No firewall, no filters on anything. I learned very quickly to read the URL carefully before hitting it and opening things after that.

We were working on the slide set. Shane was creating some basic assumptions on schedules and Wazza was putting some thought into the good and not so good aspects of the current delivery models and I was trying to shape our key messages. One of the regular staff walked up to us and asked us if we wanted red or white? I thought red or white what? Then looked up to see she had some wine glasses and two bottles of wine. One of each.

Metrolink was a dry site. No alcohol permitted on site at all, never mind consuming any and here we were on a Thursday afternoon, having a glass of wine or three and nibbles. It led into a mass departure at 5pm as the office closed and everyone decanted to the pub. It would have been rude to ignore them and so off we went onto what became our standard Thursday operating routine. Drinks in the office and then off to the pub.

The Friday morning presentation was not the most professional of my career but I made my key points and then sat down to nurse my hangover.

Serco organised lots of social events, mostly around the team but quite often there were family events too. Our first was a "Party in the Park" and took place shortly after we arrived in Melbourne. Serco had a contract to maintain all the parks and public spaces in Melbourne and held the event to celebrate a contract anniversary or contract extension, I am not quite sure. There was a marquee in Flagstaff Gardens, with a band playing, a BBQ and a drinks tent with lots of wine and ice-cold beers and a lovely sunny day.

It was my turn to be designated driver, so after a couple of beers, I went onto soft drinks. The kids joined in the footie and cricket with the other kids and Bev drank a few glasses of wine sat in the sun bronzing. However, we had no idea then, just how hot it gets and how harmful the UV rays are in Australia.

We now know that the UV rays are twice as damaging in Australia due to the hole in the ozone layer, directly above. Bev got sunburnt and was suffering from heatstroke for a good week or so and totally put her off drinking wine, even though it had little to do with it. We started to buy and slap on layers of sunblock after that Saturday in the city.

There was a bank holiday to celebrate the running of a horse race... Melbourne Cup Day, is the first Tuesday in November and nobody works. Serco had hired a massive marquee, which was plonked onto the gardens at St. Kilda and brought in outside caters. It was a mammoth event. We played cricket, touch Aussie Rules Footie, drank gallons and all put bets on the races. I don't think I have ever been anywhere in the world that has a holiday for a horse race!

The next do was the office Christmas Party and it was a little strange that Santa arrived in a red Porsche convertible, which was probably the best substitute for the lack of reindeer in the Antipodes. Serco standard marquee, band and beers. I loved working there.

I commuted Monday to Friday on the train. Within a month Saturday became just another working day and Wazza would usually pick me up and drive in as the weekend train services were limited and operated at full capacity most of the time.

My role was to lead the tram bids and provide operational input to the train bids. We had two different teams but shared some common resources, such as Scheduling, Marketing and Commercial / Financial.

Prior to 1998, the tram network had been split into two, Swanston Trams and Yarra Trams with four depot's each, plus a shared heavy maintenance depot. The 500+ trams were split across both companies. The train network had been split into three, V/Line was the country rail and feeder bus/coach services, Bayside Trains and Hillside Trains were separated from urban and suburban network.

We submitted out Indicative Bids in the first week of January. This meant working over Christmas and New Year. I worked every single day with the sole exception of Christmas Day as the client took a cheap shot and required bids to be submitted the first working day in January, knowing full well we would have to work over the festive period.

The supply chain partner responsible for printing wasn't going to be working over the festive break so we were forced into purchasing a super-dooper printer copier monster, with the free gift of a digital camera and some book binding kit, as all the submissions then were hard copy, with CD's as a back up. Not like now, with all big tender submissions via e-portals and on-line.

New Year's Day was spent proof reading and binding documents.

The following day, we got the boxes and boxes of tender documents into the client. The first bottles of fizzy, wine and beer were opened when the telephone call to confirm they had been submitted was received. We had an absolute party as a lot of tension came out for working so hard over Christmas. I didn't get home until the early hours of the morning, the following day.

Born in Stockport - Grew up in the Royal Navy

Not normally a problem, however, Bev and I had planned to take a week off and go exploring. Our plan was to drive to Sydney round the south east coast of Oz, stop at different places and see the sights. I was in no fit state to share the driving and Bev wasn't best pleased.

Bev drove all morning and most of the afternoon. Our objective was Eden, 555 kilometres away. I did offer to drive after mentally accounting for how many pints of Guinness, glasses of red wine and glasses of whisky I had drunk but Bev wouldn't have it.

We stopped for tea at a MacDonalds, the only meal that would keep the kids happy. After we dined and I drank yet another mug of tea, Beverly announced she was too tired to drive on and if I was sure it was okay, then I should complete the journey. I assured her that I was.

As I climbed into the driving seat, we had a minor fracas when Daniel spotted a redback spider on the rear windscreen. The highly venomous arachnid came off second best to the Melway. A sort of blend between an A-Z map of Melbourne and a telephone directory. It was a big fucker was the Melway and it splattered the potential invader.

Chuffed to nuts with my defence of the family, we drove out of the car parking lot, onto the highway and as we rounded the bend only a few hundred yards from Maccy D's we ran into a police road block. Bev grabbed my leg and hissed something like I hope you are alright and don't have any alcohol left in you. I said of course I will be alright but inside I did shit it a bit.

There is zero tolerance to drinking and driving in Australia, the roadblocks which were frequent, were an excellent deterrent. There were always several vehicles and usually a motorcycle or two and set in a chicane. One cop sanitises a tube and as each car stops and the window is wound down, the tube is shoved through and the driver instructed to blow. In doing so, I was the only member of our car not holding their breath.

The cop smiled, said thank you, without ever really making eye contact and waved the following car forward as we snaked between the pursuit vehicles and went on our way. It was then that Bev heaved a sigh of relief and punched my leg shouting don't ever do that to me again! Seemed a reasonable request which I have largely kept to.

On the drive round to Eden, Bev and the kids spotted kangaroos in the wild but I never did. I did see, however, a litany of dead carcasses of wombats, kangaroos and other unrecognisable animal remains the victims of roadkill and did often wonder just how many animals met their fate on the highways and byways of Australia.

Eden was gorgeous. Lovely beaches, clear blue water and lots of friendly people. The apartment we booked was in a complex with a pool. A must for our little family. Every place we booked whenever we were travelling there, had to have a pool.

It was something the kids looked forward to and something to break up the monotony of driving long distances and cries of "Are we there yet?" could be responded to with, you can spend as much time in the pool as you want, when we get there. And they did. Often staying in long after all their fingers went wrinkly, the tell-tale sign of old that you need to get out of the water and get dried.

We had two lovely days there and then drover a much shorter 200km drive to Batemans Bay, which also looked picturesque. However, the caravan we had booked turned out to be a bug-ridden wreck, looking like it belonged on the set of Jurassic Park and we refused to take it. There was a minor scene at the gate when they refused to lift the barrier but sense prevailed when I threatened to call the police and we chucked the caravan keys to them as we sped through the gate.

The rest of our arrival day was spent touring a variety of motels until we found one that had vacancies and an all-important pool for the kids to practice their Moscow State Circus balancing act in the water. Nicola on Jamie's shoulders, on Daniel's shoulders.

We managed a walk round a huge old-fashioned circus and fairground on the beach before nightfall and it was Jamie's eleventh birthday the following day, he was given the choice of what activities would make up our programme. He elected for a Maccie D's and day at the fairground and beach. A great choice.

However, it was all undermined by the torrential rainstorm we all woke up to. We did try the fair, briefly. Only to find it had now become a muddy bog and gave it up quickly. Plan B became an hour to at the indoor roller-skating rink amongst the growing crowds of other families also seeking dry entertainment. There was no let up and it rained stair rods all day.

Bev relented on our usual restrictions of Maccie D's and I think the kids ate breakfast, dinner and tea there that day. The monsoon conditions were not enough to spoil their evening swim, as it may have been wet but it was still very warm, so the three of them spent an hour or so in the pool, in the rain.

The following day, it was all sunny and blue skies as we made our way up the coast to Sydney, a drive of approximately 280km.

Sydney was an assault on the senses. Big, loud and heavily trafficked roads. We did drive over the Sydney Harbour Bridge but I was concentrating so much on signs and mad Aussie drivers, that I didn't really take in the sights. We stayed on the outskirts of the city in a chalet in a holiday camp. With a pool.

We had a good day out in Sydney and went there via a ferry from Paramatta. I liked it but the kids were bored silly. We managed a family photo with the bridge and opera house in the background. Box ticked.

Our original itinerary did include a sidestep over to the capital, Canberra and then down to Eden via Queanbeyhan but the kids got fractious and we cut the journey short as quick as we could. It was still a 550km drive though and as we came down off the mountains, it was Bev's turn to drive.

We joined a long queue on the highway and realised that the police had a big roadblock on. Lots and lots of police, with cars filing into two queues for the breathalyser. By the time we crawled up to the point where it was our turn, the air conditioning of open windows was not providing enough coolant to the three hot, sticky revolutionaries in the back seat who were making their feelings known that they were fed up of being cooped up and were kicking off.

The police officer looked into the car at all the noise and gave us sympathetic looks that probably indicated he too was a parent. He shoved the sanitised tube in front of Bev, who pursed her lips and blew into it. Great he said, now can I see your driving licence please? Bev looked at me. The cop looked at me, at the map on my lap and the three loud Stockport accented junior union officials who were demanding their right to fresh air, a MacDonald's and a pool or a beach and said, "On holiday?" Which in god's honest truth we were.

He went on "Left your licence in the hotel with your passports?" technically untrue but close enough, so we nodded. He looked at the kids and the map again and made a decision. "Go on, get those kids to the beach" and waved us on. My Aussie colleagues couldn't believe it and it was news to us, that it is compulsory to carry your driving licence as ID at all times. An instant and on the spot fine of $200 evidently. Not paid by the Perkins due to a sympathetic, if slightly misguided police officer. Thank you.

Serco's bids were pretty accurate looking back but not spectacular or as risky as the competition who won those tenders and subsequently failed to deliver some over-promising increases in patronage and revenue. I didn't know that as reaching the new year, we had some academic challenges on the horizon that changed our family focus.

Born in Stockport - Grew up in the Royal Navy

Had we been in England, Jamie would have been preparing to leave primary education and move on to secondary school. Daniel would have to choose the subjects that he would take through to GCSE courses and examinations.

We made contact with the Alexandra Park Primary School head teacher, who was amazing and sent a massive pack of exam papers and study material for Jamie, which we tried our best to work through with him.

There was no guarantee we would win the bids and though I was committed to staying if we won and wanted to take on the challenge of a senior role there, we made a family decision to return to the UK in order that Jamie and Daniel could have the best start if the bids failed.

I discussed it with the Bid Director, a lovely guy called Liam McFadden and offered to return immediately I got the family home, but he thought the best of both worlds was for me to go home with my family and remain there but support the team by working similar office hours and joining in all the reviews and teams' meetings by conference call. So that is what we did.

We had time for a long weekend at Lakes Entrance and the adorable Abel Tasman apartments, where we did a bit of boating. Puttering along in a little cabin cruiser on the Lakes and a hair-raising stint in the hotel's free hobby cat that the boys negotiated with the apartment's manager.

The guy kitted the two boys and me out with life jackets. Walked us over to his hobby cat and asked if I had sailed before? We had just sat on the rope netting in between the big floats and as I said yes but not for a long, long time, he said, "You never forget" and shoved us off from the beach without another word.

To be fair, you can't really go that wrong with a hobby cat, everything is connected on loops, the double rudders and the sail. Within minutes, I had found my balance and we raced it up and down the lagoon in front of the apartments. Great fun.

At half-term break, Jamie announced that he would be bringing a shot putt home for the holiday so he could practice with it before resuming his athletics team training on return from the break. We said yeh, sure you are. But he did.

Can you imagine a school in the UK allowing a child of eleven or any age for that matter, to bring home a 3kg metal ball to play with? We were just pleased he wasn't as good with a javelin, imagine that? I remember lugging the thing down to the local park and ensuring that we had no-one within any distance of us and watched Jamie practice with the shot putt until he got tired, or bored, or both and I lugged it back home again.

Aussie critters are definitely a step up from what we experience in the urban environment at home. Summer nights used to be disturbed by randy possums shagging on our roof and sometimes tumbling off into the bush. Cicadas were incessantly noisy and didn't trouble the kids until they saw a dead one and realised just how big they were. The size of a small starling.

Nicola used to go to bed first as the youngest (aged 8) and went into the bathroom to brush her teeth one night and our television viewing was interrupted by her piercing shriek. I honestly thought that someone had broken into our house and was attacking her until the ten big steps it took me to get there discovered there was not human intruder but there was a giant arachnid. A huntsman spider, clinging to the ceiling in the corner of the bathroom.

I like spiders, they eat bugs and my standard routine was to get a dry whisky glass, cover the spider and then slide a card between the wall or ceiling and its legs, capturing it. Then I would walk outside and shake it into the garden. Not with this one. My whisky glass would not even cover part of its body, never mind its legs. So, I shouted for Daniel to go get the fruit bowl. Which he did. And a foolscap folder. I managed to circle the spider and its legs with the bowl and slide in the folder.

When I went outside to throw the spider into the garden, Bev and the 3 kids stood there shaking their heads. So, I walked across the road and threw the spider into someone else's garden before they would let me back into the house. It was massive.

We did have a small huntsman spider that lived in our mailbox, I named Harry after a fudge advert from the 1980's. No-one would collect the mail, only me. The routine was to bang the wooden mailbox and then rustle the mail inside. Often this would be enough for Harry to retreat into a corner or up into the little apex roof of the mailbox but sometimes it wasn't. The next step was to shake the bundle of letters and mailshot adverts, furiously to dislodge him and normally that was enough. Once he made it all the way into the house and crawled out between the letters as I got through the door. A quick step back and heavy shake, then he would be off across the lawn. He made it back to the mailbox every time because he was there, every single day until we left in the April.

Our final encounter with the venomous and non-venomous critters occurred in one of our last weekends. We went for a drive down the Mornington peninsula and it was my intent for a day on the beach, then a ferry across the mouth of Port Phillip Bay from Sorrento to Queenscliff and a drive round from Geelong and St. Kilda, back to Blackburn as a full day out.

The car was a Mitsubishi Lancer, I purchased for $10,000 (c£4,000) that Serco gave me. The deal I did with the Rail MD was that I paid for tax, fuel and maintenance from my weekly allowance. At the end of the stay, to sell the car and give the money back to Serco. I sold the car to Lawrence Norton for his daughter, the day before we flew home for $8,000 (just over £2,600), which the Rail MD promptly gave me as a bonus for going out to Oz. Good man.

As we loaded up the car that Sunday morning, Nicola gave her spider scream, which got all our attention and there sat in the sill was a massive Huntsman spider. I wafted it with the Melway and it disappeared. The crew climbed in and we stowed the beach towels, cooler box with picnic in, lots of cold drinks and snacks etc. and set off.

We made good time on the coast road past our favourite beaches at Frankston, where we had taken a little table-top tinsel covered artificial tree to celebrate Christmas Day on the beach and on down to Sorrento Front Beach.

The car park we selected right next to the beach was completely empty. To be fair, the Aussies don't go anywhere near the beach until it has properly warmed up to 25 degrees plus. We would be there at any time from 18 degrees upwards, retreating to shade and air-conditioning when the beaches became Aussiefied.

As we disembarked, the spider scream was emitted from little Nicola and I had to admire the Huntsman spider's tenacity of holding onto the bottom of the door on that journey. A full swipe with the Melway saw it hit the asphalt and move off. We could hear its little feet clicking on the tarmac. I shouted something like right, it has gone, let's go and no-one moved.

I had to drive the car to the furthest side of the car park and carry out a theatrical examination of the outside of the car before anyone got out.

We lugged the chairs, wind break, cooler box and sports bag out onto the narrow strip of beach between the promenade wall and edge of the blue water. Hardly a person in sight, it was idyllic. "Uh oh", said Daniel and I thought what now. He pointed to the sausage shaped translucent cylinders covering the beach. I asked him what they were and he talked about some form of poisonous mollusc his class had been briefed on by his teacher and I thought what is it about this country? Everything wants to kill and eat you.

I got the cricket bat and spent about twenty minutes scraping a see-through-sausage free area we could sit on and batted them to one side. I went further and created a pathway all the way down to the water. Satisfied I had done the man thing, I returned to base camp and pulled a cold beer out of the cooler and pulled the ring. I don't think I got beyond one mouthful when the kids complained that the seabed was full of the pesky little sausages.

I couldn't think of any sensible or safe way to deal with that and so I reluctantly said, we are going to have to find another beach. Though I knew not where. At that moment there are three or four kids walking towards us, picking up the sausages and throwing them at each other. They sausages were either non-poisonous or these kids were mad. So, I decided to ask them what they were throwing and one of the kids said "water bombs" and I laughed. Within minutes, our kids were playing with them and they were racing up and down the beach picking armfuls up to throw at each other. Hilarious.

I settled down to finish my beer when a red light on the end of the little beach jetty started flashing and a siren went off. Shortly followed by a helicopter overhead and a large yellow inflatable boat skimming into view and one of the guys on board had a loud hailer shouting for everyone to get out of the water.

Then we saw the fin of a very large shark enter our field of vision as it patrolled the shallows. Not sure if its intended meal was sausages or little people, either way, without the chance of going back into the sea, the kids got bored and we packed up to head for the ferry, long round journey and the promise of a Maccy D's for tea.

The flight home in April 1999 was pretty seamless, other than a slight embarrassment at the flight check in desk when we discovered that Australia had unilaterally declared a 32kg limit on a single suitcase. Although that is now a world-wide standard, it was new to us. We had to unpack three cases and put all the contents into large cardboard boxes, that were then taped shut. Then spread out the clothes and other stuff to get each bag under 32kg. Not the thing you see every day in a Business Class queue.

Arriving home was a shock. It was a bit cold and wet. Bev burst into tears as she thought England looked so dirty in comparison to where we had lived for nine months and the children all burst into tears as they wanted to go back.

I continued to work on the bid, operating a sort of lunchtime to midnight, often until much later, in order to keep up with trimming cost out of the solution and then writing about it. The kids went back to school with some surprising outcomes.

Daniel came home from the session on subject choices for GCSE and announced that the teachers had employed a priority system aimed at rewarding attendance. Those with the lowest attendance were last in the queue. I remember thinking shit, he hasn't been there. However, the beaming Daniel went on to say it was down to absences and he hadn't been there, so didn't have any absences recorded against him. Bonus. He got all his subject choices.

The body blows started arriving as the Victoria State Treasury Department chose the wildly optimistic bids over Serco and we lost out on all five franchises. It was no consolation to know that most of them failed miserably calling for the government to create new arrangements within only a couple of years. We didn't win.

We were already returning to Melbourne in our hearts and minds. We had the house valued, checked on our limited investments and insurances and had an emigration plan ready to activate. It was therefore no surprise to know that all five us were devasted that we would not be going back. We would never just go on a whim, we needed guaranteed work for me or we wouldn't go.

Our Australia Adventure therefore came to an end but it did take us all some time to get it out of our system.

I remember being sat outside in a beer balcony, at a very sunny Blackpool, the second or third weekend in June 1999 when I got a call on my mobile that we had lost the last bid. We were in Blackpool for the RailSport Games, the annual event for rail companies to test their prowess in a number of competitive challenges. We went there to play 5 a-side football. But more of that later.

1999 was also the year a whole bunch of us from Metrolink started going to Dublin for a weekend of drinking and silly fun. Mainly lads who had been in the services. We started off using proper hotels but within a few years, had degenerated into using a hostel that was one building back from the famous Temple Bar, in the Temple Bar district, Dublin 1.

Ten of us in bunk beds, two toilets and one shower. It was mad. The favourite route was the high-speed ferry from Liverpool to Dún Laoghaire (pronounced Dunn Leery) and a coach or minivan into Dublin, drinking all the way. Though we also used RyanAir and flew in a few times as well. Great fun.

Chapter Fifteen

The RailSport Games at Blackpool

Born in Stockport - Grew up in the Royal Navy

All told I went to Blackpool for 17 consecutive games from 1997 before I gave it up. By then we had won numerous football medals as winners or runners-up and made valiant efforts to drink Blackpool dry but never quite managed it.

Anarchic weekends that probably peaked in 2011 when we achieved total domination and won the Veteran over 35's event, whilst operating a BBQ and consumed a chest cooler box (the size of a small coffin) full of beer. It was hilarious.

Unlike on some previous years when we had battled the inclement weather, that weekend it was gloriously sunny, well it was on the Friday and Saturday. Ian Law had set out on the Friday morning by driving his estate car to Blackpool and parked it in the Recreation Centre at Stanley Park, the HQ for the events. Then he caught the train back to Manchester to rendezvous with the rest of us in the pub at lunchtime.

The car held windbreaks, a BBQ set and the gigantic cooler box that he had painstakingly filled with several crates of canned lager and beer and buckets of ice. Plus, a traditional can of Special Brew that was the punishment prize for mistake of the day. That can was always removed from the cooler and left to fester in the sun all day. The perpetrator of the worst mistake of the day had to down it in one later on...

Friday was a full drinking day. At an agreed time, we would board the train from Piccadilly to Blackpool, complete with a carry out of beer, some entertainment of cards and dice and off we would go to cause havoc with the commuters leaving town and heading home across the northwest to Blackpool. This one was no different.

Born in Stockport - Grew up in the Royal Navy

Standard routine was to check into whichever cheap bed and breakfast would entertain a huge, well about a dozen, drunken lads. In all honesty, they were booked in advance and the hosts knew full well what they were letting themselves in for.

This year's hostel of choice was used to hosting stag weekends and the place had a minimalist overall design of leather chesterfields, telly's and a bar with lots of offers of buy 4 get 1 free and a happy hour.

Lea Harrison, our party organiser of great repute had purchased loads of bottles of Stella Artois, on offer, to be served ice cold with our breakfast at the same hotel the year before. Now as much as we all like a beer, it is hard trying to force one down with your sausage, egg, bacon and beans but we did.

This year, one or two of the horses had refusals at this particular fence and concentrated on the fresh orange juice, served in large jugs full of ice. To which Lea kept saying cheers. Those of us that could stomach an ice-cold Stella, did both and all the time little Lea keeps saying cheers.

It was only when we got into Yates when it opened at 11am that he revealed, with the hotel owner's consent and complicity, that he had poured half a bottle of vodka into the three jugs of orange juice. Outstanding.

We couldn't work out why Snakey missed breakfast, then we could as his mouth displayed the fight he lost with the urinal he collapsed onto and spend time in A&E having it sutured. He spent the rest of the weekend sipping his beer through a straw poor lad.

We all then got changed into a yellow and black football kit, which would be the dress of the day until we returned in the evening.

Before we got to Yates wine bar, Glenn (Mr Alcohol himself) Kelly, needed to have his annual dip in the not so lagoon-like waters of Blackpool North Shore and shot off across the beach (the tide was out) chased by Tony (Mr Angry) Martin, stripping off their kit as they ran.

It was a bit boring watching them run the two hundred miles or so out to where the brown foam lashed waves that signified the Irish Sea started, so the rest of us trudged off to Yate's playing "keepy uppy" with our only football.

We were joined in Yates a short while later by the now very damp Kelly and TM. Once they had got a beer organised, Kelly started to tell a story about thrashing about in the waves, he had encountered a monster fish from the ocean deep. He described how it had accosted him and he feared for his life then like a magician pulling a rabbit out of a hat, whipped a big brown jelly fish out of his shorts and slapped it onto the tabletop with a big wet SLOP sound.

Cue pandemonium as players feared losing their drinks and grabbed their bottles amid howls of laughter and something else. A noise of fear. Cossie fatally revealed that he was frightened of jelly fish. With several nods and winks, along with some guidance from a very large doorman, the jelly fish was secured into a plastic carrier bag for Ron. Later on.

We would usually get a carry out, jump into taxi's and head for Stanley Park. This year, however, we only needed one beer each for the taxi journey, as a great feast awaited us in the Lawmans car.

Ian had loaded the coffin, beer by beer, then added some bacon, sausage, burgers and baps before cramming all the available gaps with ice. It was a different story trying to lift it out of the car and carry it down to the pitch. Four lads to lift and carry, the rest got the BBQ set, makings and two wind break sets.

The competition rules clearly stated no alcohol pitch side, so we located our base strategically opposite the organisers tent but directly outside of the gate to the chain-link fenced off football pitches.

As it was sunny, the ground was hard and it was difficult to get the wind break posts in position. Rochy jogged over to the stadium where some athletes had been using the track and field and borrowed a shot putt. It was ideal for hammering the posts into the ground. I asked him if he was going to return it but Rochy said it was a "Manchester Borrow" meaning it may not get back to them.

Whilst the burgers, sausages and bacon are being cooked on the BBQ for our lunch and the first course of ice-cold beer is being consumed, someone suggested that we have a shot putt throwing competition, to one side of the pitches. The worst throw would lead to a penalty of wearing the jelly fish as a wig for half an hour.

Cossie was the only person who didn't work out that his throw would be the worst. No matter how far he threw it. We were in fits of giggles as the competitive Cossie disagreed with the judge's verdict on where his shot putt had landed. His protestations were waved away and he tried again, and again. When the penny finally dropped, Cossie did no more than grab the carrier bagged jellyfish and run off to the other side of Stanley Park to hide it from us.

Cossie was by far the fastest of us and so other than a token chase that probably lasted no more than two seconds, we left him to run away and collapsed in fits of laughter. Then went back to the base for more beer.

We ate the burgers, some with cheese on, bacon and sausage butties as athletes from other teams were warming up and stretching all around us. We just drank more beer.

During some competitive games in the sun, we won them all, topped our group and would return for the knockout stages on the following day. At this point, the sensible thing to do would be an athlete's night in and perhaps watch the telly after a nice evening meal. Not us.

The BBQ kit had cooled. Ged had knocked back the warm bubbly Carlsberg Export for miss of the day and all the windbreaks and cool box were stowed back in the Lawmans estate car. We then moved on to our standard pub crawl. Our first stop was The Belle Vue, then across the road to The Guards Club, a private ex-HM Forces social club, members only that we had stumbled on years before.

Born in Stockport - Grew up in the Royal Navy

Either Lea or I would sign everyone in as visitors and then we set to with the cheap prices. We would normally play silly drinking games, with the failure penalty, some concoction we decided was worthy, or drink half a pint, whilst playing killer on the darts board and snooker table.

The staff in their loved us going in as we drank loads, were very respectful of their club and then we would move on to the front. Usually, the Tower Lounge and drink with all the stag and hen parties who mobbed the place.

Before it got dark, we would head back to get changed and eat on the run in the form of fish and chips or a kebab. Quick shower, shufty and shave, then it was back out into the festival of drinking and try not to get into trouble.

Sunday seemed to appear from no-where, as did some nasty grey clouds depositing gallons of water in the form of rain. So, after a hearty breakfast, with not that much alcohol, we made our way back to Stanley Park and somehow got through and won the final. The medal ceremony had to take place in the gym due to the inclement weather.

Despite our best efforts, we were never to win the competition again, though we did reach the semi-finals on a number of occasions. The over 35's were getting increasingly younger each year and the organisers could not be persuaded to opening an over 45's competition. Still, we tried.

Kelly brought his mate, Jimmy Quinn one year. Jimmy being the former Northern Ireland international, capped 46 times for his country and an absolute legend in our little history with the RailSport Games. He had played with Kelly at Whitchurch Alport and Congleton Town as a youngster and they had remained friends ever since.

Jimmy joined in with our silly drinking games and introduced us all to "Captain Thumb" a subtle and damning game that we would include in amongst other drinking games to cause confusion and increase the error rate, which of course, increased the alcohol intake of those making said mistakes.

He also brought with him some horse tips and with his expert (or very lucky) predictions, won us about £300 to add to our drinking kitty for the weekend. Good lad.

Hammy won the warm Carlsberg Export can when he was lobbed after acting as a sweeper / keeper. Lea has never let him forget and always says that Hammy, big man that he is, was lobbed in the Subbuteo nets of the 5 a-side pitch. Despite Hammy objecting that he was nearly on the halfway line when the fateful lob took place. Even so, it's still funny.

I was still playing for Metrolink, long after I finished working there. We were the oldest team by far and getting older each year, whilst the opposition was getting younger. Two trajectories that only have one ending and we stopped going.

Chapter Sixteen

David

It was during my time at Metrolink, the tram network in Greater Manchester, that my brother David's illness started to reach a peak. Some years before he had some odd consecutive ailments. He had a growth on his neck and his knee became infected and now he was in hospital with pneumonia. His friend Deborah had told me that David was ill and in Bolton General hospital in a separate ward, which I also thought was odd. I got the call late at night and remember lay in bed talking to Beverly about it. I was on early shift next morning and so agreed to go straight from work to Bolton.

When I got to the hospital, staff attending David were wearing face masks and gloves, which confirmed what I thought. David said that he had something to tell me and started sobbing. I sat beside him and held his hand and said that I already knew. David said to let him continue, he found this difficult enough.

Born in Stockport - Grew up in the Royal Navy

David said he had something to tell me and I said again that I knew. David said that he was gay, and I said I know David, I have known you were gay since you were very young and that isn't what you need to tell me is it? By now we were both in floods of tears and David told me he was HIV positive.

He didn't know how to tell our Mum and Dad. I agreed that I didn't know either but I knew one thing, he could not tell them lay in a hospital bed with a drip in his arm and staff wandering around wearing rubber gloves and face masks. He would get better and choose the right moment. He did.

David had qualified from Canterbury Christ Church University with honours and with just a little more study would be able to title himself Professor, just as the bullies at Offerton Hall school had so many years before. He struggled for a while to get his first teaching job and eventually settled on a difficult inner-city school in Stratford, a very rough and tough part of East London.

The disease would attack the weakest parts of his body first – the knee was where he had damaged it on the construction site of the estate all those years before and he was told in a very direct style by the GP treating him, that his eyesight would be next and it was likely that he would go blind before he died. Evidently it was said as brutally as that and I know that it upset David.

A prolific reader and someone who adored writing and receiving correspondence with family and friends, it would be a serious blow to his mental health and well-being..

David worked out he needed to be nearer home and the support of our family but we of course were unaware at the point that David said he had bought a property in Oldham and would we help him move to a new house. David would become a supply teacher in Oldham and take things from there.

This all took place before we spoke in that isolation ward in Bolton hospital.

Born in Stockport - Grew up in the Royal Navy

My bezzy oppo Paul Finch, our Ged and me were to be the moving crew because David could not afford the extortionate fee's being quoted by removal firms. I hired a Ford Transit Luton Van from the cheapest van hire place I could find, Mitchells on the A6 in Stockport Town Centre. For a 24-hour hire period for a dash south, a load up and a dash back north.

The van hire was 1200noon one day and return by 1200noon the next day. Paul and I were on rest days and Ged wasn't in school. So off we went, with Paul and me sharing the driving down to East London and then back up to Oldham. I don't think we really knew what we were letting ourselves in for but would soon find out.

David had warned us that East London was a tough place. His tales of vandalism, theft and muggings seemed to be a daily occurrence on the not-so-charming garden estate of tower blocks on Carpenters Road, Stratford. We went armed with claw hammers and wood staves, in the van 3-seater cab and placed in the Luton body. Just in case.

The council flat that David occupied had been "sold" to him a few years previously. Seemed the routine was you pay the tenant a fee as a sort of deposit, the tenant then adds you to the rent agreement as a co-tenant for six months prior to the transfer. At the point of transfer, you "buy" the rent book for a final payment and six months later, scratch off the previous tenant and hey presto, you are now the "owner" of a council flat, complete with a rent book.

David had told of us the incident where the previous tenant, another teacher, returned to collect some final belongings and had parked in the resident's car park at the rear of the tower block. David had raised his concern but she said it would only be there for a few minutes but that is all it took. When she returned to her car she found the roof collapsed in as someone had dropped a concrete paving stone from the top of the tower block onto her car.

When we arrived at the tower block in the early evening, David suggested reversing up on to the footpath so the entrance overhang roof, overlapped the back of the Luton Van. That's when the noises started. Someone on the top of the tower block was dropping marbles or ball bearings and they pinged off the light alloy roof of the hire van.

Born in Stockport - Grew up in the Royal Navy

It took no more than three quarters of an hour to move David's stuff from the pile he had prepared outsides his flat, into the van. We took possession of the lift as it moved between the 19th floor and ground zero where our transport was under attack.

Loaded up we managed to dodge any missiles that may have been thrown at us and followed David in his Ford Capri out through the joys of East London in the dark and headed north. It was only as we loaded up that David announced due to some repairs, his speed would be limited to fifty miles per hour. It took all night to drive north and get him unloaded in Oldham, which we did after a full English breakfast somewhere on our travels.

I dropped off Paul and Ged, then with David, made one more journey from Oldham back to Stockport where he had some stuff stored in Uncle Albert's garage. It was late morning when I finally left Oldham to drive the van back to Mitchells on the A6 and I had to drive carefully as I had been on the go for twenty-four hours.

I stood with the guy checking the van back in, willing him not to look up at the pock marked roof above us. He signed it in and I strolled home and went to bed. Completely knackered.

David held a housewarming party, he also cooked a meal for Paul, Judy, Bev and me as a way of saying thank you for our endeavours and chose an evening when Mum, Dad and our Ged could go round for him to tell them his predicament.

I remember my Dad being very angry. He wanted to know who had turned David gay. It was a thing he and Mum didn't really understand. They tolerate homosexuality but find it odd and they have no idea that someone doesn't "turn" they just are who they are.

In saying that, when the shit hit the fan, they were amazingly supportive at a time in the late 1980's when the whole subject of HIV and AIDS generated hysteria by the media, hate and distrust by the community and great misunderstanding even within the health service.

As a family, we chose to keep it to ourselves and didn't discuss the subject or our David, with anyone else.

Born in Stockport - Grew up in the Royal Navy

David was on holiday in Crete, staying with an old friend from University and her family. He was on his way home and was in the transfer to the airport when he noticed something wrong. His eyes started to go foggy and by the time he got into the airport concourse his eyesight had gone. All he could see that day were silhouettes and he had a panic attack.

With help, he managed to board the flight and called Mum and Dad from Manchester Airport on arrival. The flight and ground staff were incredibly helpful in getting him on and off the plane and through the terminals to the waiting arms of Mum and Dad, who then drove him home. His sight never returned.

It was a difficult time and he received support from the Teachers Union and was eventually pensioned off. He had to sell his house in Oldham and moved to a ground floor flat in a housing association complex back in Stockport, where he received support to learn the layout, brew up and make simple meals. We discussed the challenge of taking on a guide dog but it wasn't practical as the clock was now ticking on David's time with us.

It was a brain tumour that caused the blindness and ultimately contributed to his passing.

To watch a brilliant mind, handsome man and bright light in the community fade away was harrowing for all of us. He had played cupid for Beverly and me. He had taught so many children the joys of English Literacy and reading. He regularly communicated with a vast array of friends from work, from his social life and across our large family. He had a knack of getting people together.

David was poorly with some flu like symptoms and so he temporarily moved back in with Mum and Dad and was supported once a day by a lovely care worker. He had got up in the middle of the night to go to the loo. In his flat he knew to turn right into the bathroom. At Mum and Dads, he turned right and fell down the stairs and broke his arm.

After it was set, his stay at home with Mum and Dad became a fixed one after thieves broke into his flat and robbed it. We will never really know what they took in the form of jewellery and precious things because they trashed the flat as well and David was struggling to describe what was what and where it was.

As the pain from the brain tumour increased, David was prescribed ever increasing amounts of oral morphine that he took at home and left him semi-conscious at times. It was no surprise when the doctor suggested it was time to move into hospital.

David was placed into Monsall Isolation hospital in North Manchester. It is a business park now but then it was Manchester's dedicated isolation hospital and had been so since 1954.

The Metrolink HQ was less than a mile away in Collyhurst. I chose to tell my boss, the Traffic Manager, that my brother was terminal and ensconced in Monsall Hospital just over the way. He said that whenever I was on duty and mobile, that I could spend some time with him and did so most days. I had a radio and could be called away to respond to incidents as and when. No-one else at work knew and as far as they were concerned, I was "mobile".

David wasn't responsive in those last days, he was just lay in bed almost coma-like. One day I was there and got called on the radio. I had been holding his hand and said I had to go. I told him I was going to miss him and he squeezed my hand. The last time I got anything from him in this world.

It was either that night or the following night, the hospital called us all in and said it looked like it was time. To wake up I had a wash and brushed my teeth. Then I got in my car and drove over from Edgeley. It took about twenty-five minutes.

It would be less if it was today as there is now a dual carriageway through East Manchester but back then it was a series of traffic signalled junctions as demolition of the old factories and stuff was underway.

It was when I was sat at the fourth or fifth junction away from the hospital at yet another red light, that I felt something. I can only describe it as someone passing a piece of metal through my body. It caught my breath and held me so for a good few second's. I could also smell steel, which was odd. Then the feeling left me, the lights had changed to green and I pressed on to Monsall Hospital.

The staff who let me in said I was just a few minutes too late. He had already left us. It was then I thought that David had let me know he was gone when I was sat at those traffic lights. I have no other explanation for my feelings.

I made my way into the ward to find Mum, Dad and Ged around David's bed all crying.

We made arrangements for the funeral and it was only then did we explain to the rest of our family and friends what had happened. Bouquets of flowers poured in from near and far away, so much so that the smell of fresh flowers to this day, still reminds Mum of David's funeral.

Ged and I had taken on the task of informing all of David's friends, most of whom we had never met. So, it was a sobering process cold calling with the sad news. We had divvied up his address book but after two or three days, there was still a small cadre of numbers that we hadn't been successful in calling in the evening and decided to meet up at Mum and Dads for support and make some daytime calls.

The format was the same for everyone. Hello, you don't know me but I am Ged/Moz, David's brother and we have some sad news to tell you, he has passed away. Then we would share the funeral details and the person would either say they would be attending or not and ask for an address where cards/flowers could be sent.

We got to Gordon Ford, where neither of us had been able to make contact previously. It was my turn and the phone was picked up. Is that Gordon Ford? Yes, I am Moz, David Perkins brother and we have some sad new to tell you, he has passed away. The voice on the other end said, I am very sorry to hear that, but this is Gordon Ford, the Ford dealership in Hazel Grove.

A light moment, at a very, very sad time for us all.

Born in Stockport - Grew up in the Royal Navy

Almost 30 years on, it still hurts. Just not as much as it did then. His birthday and the date of his passing are etched on our Mum and they become her grieving days for him though I know she thinks about him every day. I miss him immensely.

Daniel and Jamie have some slight memories of David, mostly brought back from looking at old photographs. They do remember his giant bird eating frogs that he kept in his back garden in Oldham and his little fishpond. Nicola wasn't quite two years old when he passed away on 23rd June 1992 and doesn't have any memory of him.

Chapter Seventeen

Family holidays

Before our children were born, holidays were few and far between. We had deferred our honeymoon for two years and had a Thomson package holiday to Majorca in 1982. Other than that, holidays were confined to camping in those early years as we had no money.

I had only been camping with Mum and Dad a couple of times before I went in the Navy and would never say that I was experienced. Never more so than when I came home on leave and borrowed their tent and some other basic stuff and went camping with mates from Stockport down in Cornwall in 1975.

Ten of us in three cars for a booze filled barmy week. My key problem was breaking two ribs and flattening my lung playing football in Faslane, when I was HMS Antrim. I didn't usually play in goal unless our keeper was injured but in this case it was me. Hatch rash (failing to step up over hatch housings) had caused two or three big scabby lumps on my shins. I went down to sickbay to grab some cotton wool to wad out and protect me behind my shin pads.

However, the vet wanted to know why I needed the cotton wool and so showed him my shins. He applied some local anaesthetic and sliced off the scabs with a scalpel to reveal I had three infected holes. He sprayed them with something antiseptic, used for dressing flash burns, taped them up and signed me on light duties for three days and no football. Right.

I grabbed some cotton wool when he wasn't looking, stuffed them in my shin pads and went off to play for the mess. In a moment of sensibility when I discussed with Ali Kennedy the team captain and key striker, that I best go in nets and not go crunching into tackles with my injured shins.

When I punched a ball out from a corner and was hit by the opposing centre forward who then kindly kneed me in the back as we fell to the ground and I lay there winded, it didn't seem such a sensible move.

Ali called for the sub and I was dragged off the pitch still barely breathing, lay against a chain link fence and the game carried on. It was posh Scouse Chadwick that spotted I was in trouble when I refused his offer of a can of Carlsberg Export that he thought I may be ill and called an ambulance.

Blues and Twoohs going, I was rushed into the remarkably well stocked sick bay at Faslane. Something to do with supporting the submariners I guess and a duty doctor. He laughed when he saw my X-Rays and commented how distorted my rib cage was. Broke one playing football the year before and the epic fall from the rope swing as a kid no doubt.

He put me on morphine for twenty-four hours. Not the oral shit but something intravenous. I sort of glided into the ward where I was put for a few days across the way from my buddy Bilbo, who had glandular fever and shouted that it was nice of me to visit him. Funny fucker. He loaned me a book of funny rugby stories, as much to see and hear me whinge when I laughed more than anything else.

The following week, we were back in Pompey and I began my summer leave by surprising Mum and Dad with my request to borrow their tent. Didn't get the letter I didn't write evidently.

Travelling light, none of us took anything padded to lie on and just dropped our sleeping bags onto the ground sheet. A mistake I was never going to make again. I don't think I slept much as the broken ribs took some time to heal. Still, we had a great week fishing for mackerel, teaching the locals how to play Don and drinking gallons of ale.

Born in Stockport - Grew up in the Royal Navy

So, getting back to cheap family holidays. In 1983, Pete and Anne Ford, had their two boys Matthew and James and saw camping as a low-cost solution. Bev and I started off borrowing Mum and Dad's tent and took our Ged and Paul Finch with us. We camped near Rhyl the first time and only decided to go at the last minute on a Friday evening in autumn.

It was going dark and starting to rain when we got to the campsite and shove the big frame tent up as quickly as we could before retiring to the dry inside and then opening a can of kestrel lager each. Some bits of string were irritating me as I drank my can and it was then I realised that we had put the tent up inside out. Brilliant.

The next day when it had dried out, we quickly took off the outer tent, turned it the right way round and shoved it back on before anyone really noticed.

The next time, we took Bev's sister Christine and her two boys with us and had three tents on a stony filed in Penmaenmawr, just off the A55 and it rained almost the entire weekend.

Every time we went away, we would see other campers with different levels of experience and different bits of kit. We always referred to them as "Proper Campers" and in fact it became a saying with us to describe almost anyone, with anything, in any situation where there had gadgets or smarter ways of doing things. Both families bought large frame tents as a result.

After our successful weekends in and around North Wales, we planned a proper expedition for our summer holiday in 1984 and headed south to Slapton Sands, in Devon for a week and then five days in Minehead in Somerset. This is where we were re-introduced to cider. Not the bottled stuff we used to buy but draught cider, cloudy cider and very strong.

Knowing how notoriously bad the congestion could get around Birmingham, our plan included a night drive down to the south west and we set off just after midnight for a leisurely drive down. We were all big Citizen Band radio enthusiasts and each had a rig in our cars, so we kept contact throughout the journey, with some funny stories and jokes being told as we made our way south. The little ones slept through most of it.

Born in Stockport - Grew up in the Royal Navy

On arrival, we pitched the tents and went out to explore and found a lovely little pub in the village selling strong draught cider. Excellent.

Pete loved a drink. We all did but it was a particular thing for Pete and he would leap into action at the merest hint of one.

Camp duties were always split between us, who cooked, who washed the pots and that sort of thing. We had forgotten who was doing what and were just chilling after our tea and in the lovely warm evening when Anne reminded Pete that it was the boys turn to wash the pots. "Oh are?" said Pete, without moving, when Anne added that once the pots were done, we could get off to the pub. It was like someone had thrown 5,000 volts through Peter.

He jumped up, grabbed the buckets full of dirty pots and shouted at his son's, Ged and me to get a move on over to the sinks at the wash block "Quickly, Quickly" was his encouraging shout to mobilise us all. Words that have also become lodged into our vocabulary and used when we need things to hurry up.

I managed to smash my spectacles on a beach, the day before we departed north to Minehead and didn't have a spare pair with me. Our default position on any problem was to call Dad. Mr Reliable. He used his set of keys to retrieve my old national health frames from home, pack them and put them in the post to the address of the campsite in Minehead. Good man.

I drove in the middle of our three-car convoy, for safety and we used the radio as much to maintain a steady speed, keep to the mapped journey and encourage me along. I was as blind as a bat without my bins on.

Thankfully we arrived in Minehead, none too worse for the wear and a little parcel containing my black rimmed spare bins to that I could magically see again.

The week down in Slapton had been all blue skies and sunny weather, lots of beach time and a little bit of exploring. However, it was all change when we got to Minehead. Grey and cloudy, with showers and drizzle. Great stuff and we were inundated with spiders. They were everywhere.

Beverly does not like anything that flies or crawls, quite amazing that she did decide in the end to go to Australia when we did, considering the Antipodes hosts some of the world's most poisonous flying and crawling things...

The routine in Minehead was to send in the men. Pete, Paul and I acted as beaters and we had to shake out all the sleeping bags in an evening, theatrically brush the inside of the inner tents and demonstrate we had removed any sign of spiders before Beverly, Anne and the kids would enter the tents.

In the morning, we awoke to spiders in every corner of the inside of the tent, on the inner tent, inside the inner tent and all over the equipment.

The evening cleansing routine was repeated in the morning as well, as we fanned, used rolled up newspapers as coshes and rid all spiders from view.

On the last morning, we only had enough makings for one breakfast sitting. Paul had used the last of the butter to fry and had already started to crack eggs into an omelette, when a rather large hairy spider became dislodged from the inside of the tent, fell on to its back in the makings and fried to a crisp in seconds. Paul and I just looked at each other and he said, "More protein, they'll never know" and stirred the crispy arachnid in with the omelette. Only Paul and I know the true story. Until I wrote this anyway.

We moved onto caravans the following year, as cheap as camping but with better home comforts. A week in Amlwch, near Holyhead on the Isle of Anglesey, may not suit everyone but the price was right for Pete, Anne with Matthew and James, along with Paul, our Ged, Bev, me and our seven-month-old son Daniel.

In a real quirk of fate, the guy who's house the single caravan was pitched on, was the best friend of one of the guys we ran with, Billy Stephenson a plumber on the council. It didn't take long to make the connection once he knew I worked for the council and he invited "the lads" to join him for his weekly boys only sports evening. He had a pool table, a dart board and a little bar where he dispensed his incredibly strong home brew beer in his garage, he had converted into a games room.

Born in Stockport - Grew up in the Royal Navy

We had a great night, playing in a little round-robin tournament at pool and darts. However, it wasn't until the guy opened his garage door at the end of the evening and fresh air flooded in that I realised how strong his home-brew beer was. I couldn't walk the hundred yards or so across his garden and into the field where the caravan was parked.

I fell over a little picket fence and for reason's know only to me, tried several times to get back over it, when we were already inside the area fenced off for the holiday let caravan. When I did get there, I managed to fall into and then out of the little bed in dining area. I finally fell soundly asleep.

When I woke up, it was well after noon. The caravan was empty as everyone had eaten breakfast but not at the dining table as I was flat out in the bed there, then they had gone out for the day. I never heard a thing.

I spent most of the day drinking water and trying to keep my eyes focussed on things. Helped considerably by the boring cricket test match being shown "live" on the little telly in the caravan. I had a lot of making up to do when everyone returned and already had a tea on the go for them all when they got back. It didn't take long.

I'm not too sure if it was the following year, or the one after but we turned our attention to renting a cottage for our big summer holiday. We chose "Mrs Jones Cottage", though that wasn't its name. I think it was called Rose Cottage but the landlady was Mrs Jones, who ran the farm it sat on, from a smaller part of the farmhouse. It was painted all white and located not far from the hamlet of Sarn Bach and a short drive to the Warren Beaches at Abersoch.

Great place for family holidays. We would have a big breakfast. Full fry up with everything whilst making a massive pile of sandwiches. Then we would load up the cars with the beach stuff and the kids and head down there for the day. Safe swimming. Beer and soft drinks in the cooler boxes and a feast of butties to come.

We would only head back to Mrs Jones when we ran out of food or the kids got fed up and / or tired, whichever came first.

We missed a day one year when the coast was hit by a massive storm. Big strong winds and heavy driving rain and we were all glad we had upped our game from camping to more substantial accommodation. Indoor games, long stories and trying to keep active kids happy was a struggle but we managed it.

The following day was all blue skies, still and sunny. Another beach day. Hurray! After a hearty breakfast we were one of the first onto the Warren Beach. We used to make our way from the car parking area, across duckboard walkways through the sand dunes and onto the beach.

Our routine was adults first to pick a spot, create the beachhead with windbreaks etc. then round up the kids, the rest of the adults, beach chairs, cooler boxes, footballs and inflatable things and join up at our beach encampment.

As we walked onto the beach, one of our usual spots was taken up by a dead deer. Sadly, it must have been washed into the sea whilst giving birth, as a fawn was half in and half out of her. A sad sight and one we didn't want to the kids to see. So, we moved a few hundred yards down the beach before returning for the main force.

Peter led the way with Matthew, James, Daniel, Jamie and others in tow, with a few adults at the rear to pick up any stragglers or things that the kids determined were too heavy to carry and had been left in the sand dunes for the beach fairies to carry. As Pete saw the deer carcases on the beach shouted at the top of his voice "Look over there, a dead deer!" and ran over to them with all the kids in tow. Cheers Pete.

Later that day, the men took the kids on a walk into Abersoch for ice creams and a sneaky pint in the pub. As we trudged through the wet sand of the little harbour Matthew found a dead dogfish that was missing its eyes. Probably eaten by the gulls.

When we got home from the holiday and grandparents enquired off our children had they had a good time. All they would recite was that they had seen a dead deer with a baby sticking out of its bum and a fish with no eyes. Magic.

We also enjoyed and still enjoy, having holidays at Center Parcs, since experiencing the first holiday park in Sherwood Forest back in 1989, a year and a bit after it first opened.

Our normal approach is to head there in a convoy of several families and also be open to host visitors who stay with us for 24 hours or so. We hire several large houses and crew up for various activities around the park.

One year, we shared with the Harrisons and next door was the Fords and Finches. Lea and I took all the boys out to play football, partly in a competition and then just between ourselves and then we went on the pop. The deal was, we would return in the evening to mind all the small kids, whilst the ladies went for a spa pampering and others went for a meal.

Lea was bumping his gums about why I had blocked his promotion at work and in our drunken babysitter state, did my best to explain. Our discussion was alcohol infused and occasionally loud. However, every half hour or so, we paused to check on how the kids were doing. Nicola and Paige having a disco in one of the bedrooms, Daniel, Jamie, Richard, Edward and Regan, were all playing a variety of computer fighting games against each other.

When everyone returned, had a chat, put the kids to bed etc. we had retired to our lodge and it was just Lea and me watching some boxing highlights that were being shown late. We had a good laugh about our drunken discussions earlier and made a bit of noise.

Beverly came out of our room and told us off, that there were babies asleep and we needed to quieten down. Then she turned on her heels and marched back to the bedroom.

Lea leaned over to me and whispered in my ear "She doesn't scare me" and I leaned back towards him and whispered, "Why are you whispering then?" which had us both laughing out loud and in tears. It is a punchline we use all across the family to this day. She doesn't scare me. LOL X.

Chapter Eighteen

Born in Stockport - Grew up in the Royal Navy

Perkins Clan

Our children Daniel, Jamie and Nicola have been a source of much fun, great worry and immense pride, as they have developed from tiny helpless babies into healthy, strapping and successful adults.

Beverly and I had to manage the same sibling rivalry that I had experienced with my brother David and I did my best to find ways to stop it but was never wholly successful. The thing that hurt me the most and still does, is that David and I only really became proper friends as brothers after we left home and we were denied a long and lasting friendship when he got ill and died. Something I threw at my children when I was in despair of stopping them arguing and fighting.

I also did what my parents did and smacked them when they were naughty. Something I regretted whenever I did it and sometimes cried. I tried so hard to be a friend as well as a father but in the face of some actions, I smacked. Once I threw Daniel the length of the bedroom after I caught him hitting Jamie and separated them. Daniel didn't stop until he hit the radiator and fell onto the carpet. A distance of about fifteen feet. I was beside myself.

We did everything with our children, something I missed out on, in terms of supporting them at Tae Kwon Do, at Football and at Gymnastics. My Dad only saw me play football as an adult and never saw me run a race, in either athletics or cross-country. He needed to work and worked every hour god sent to bring in the income and ensure we had food on the table and a roof over our heads. He did that very well.

Bev (mainly) and I drove them to classes, attended competitions and tournaments, whilst balancing work commitments and cash.

When we could go out, it was often on a budget and we used to take picnics on canal walks and when we had the time and money, occasionally drive to the coast and find a beach. In the main though, beaches were our holiday thing, rarely as a day out.

One day when we were all packed and ready, with three children safely seated and belted in the rear, there had been some cries of being desperate for food, despite the short time since breakfast and Bev had reached into her bag for a snack for each of them. Something had been spilt or smeared and responding to the cry of help, Beverly again reached into her bag for some wet wipes and sorted things out.

I said, do you know kids, your Mum is like Mary Poppins as I remembered the scene on arrival in the Banks household and Julie Andrews proceeds to pull things out of her bag with great abandon. However, my feet were put firmly on the ground when Jamie said "No she isn't. She can't fly" a statement of fact that brought the car to a stop amid howls of laughter.

Nicola was doing well at Gymnastics and dropped out of Tae Kwon Do but not before winning a trophy in her age range and belt. The boys, however, continued and both were successful in completing their black belts and went on to fight in bigger tournaments but more of that later.

Beverly got roped into helping out at Stockport School of Gymnastics and became a coach and regional competition judge but in the early days, it was all about getting the kit out at Dialstone Recreation Centre and putting it all away again.

Our house contained weights that the boys used and a pull up bar that everyone used, strategically placed in a doorway to take out foreheads of unsuspecting adults.

Nicola was very proud of her achievements and called me on the mobile on her way home with Bev to tell me of her new move. A Chinkikova. I was ecstatic and told all my work colleagues that my little nine-year-old daughter had achieved a "Chinkikova" not that I had any clue who the soviet athlete was or what the move consisted of. I obviously know Olga Korbut but very few others. I just had these images of our little girl whirling and tumbling through the air to great effect.

All became apparent, however, when Nicola explained the move that this little gymnast had learned. She was helped up to the bar by her coach, where she pulled herself up to her chin and then kicked her body backwards over the bar in a single move known as a Chin Kick Over...... right.

Jamie and Daniel fought in a number of tournaments. Jamie fought twice in the open World Championships and acquitted himself well. Daniel had an epic fight against the European champion in the British tournament and only narrowly lost to a man who seriously injured a number of other competitors. Not a game for the faint hearted that is for sure.

The problem for me was that Daniel and Jamie could bring all their training to the fore whenever it kicked off between them.

We were on holiday in France, on a beach in Brittany with the Finch family. The kids are all doing things on the beach and the adults are sharing tales and sipping continental cold beers, when something sparked off between our two boys. In only a couple of seconds they had squabbled, both settled into Tae Kwon Do stances and exchanged a number of kicks and punches before retiring back into guarding stances.

Beverly shouted at me as to why I hadn't stopped them. Stopped them, I replied, I barely saw them.

Between the three of them fighting, we have had to replace the front door lock twice and the whole door once, a windowpane in the door and the entire studded wall between the boys bedrooms that was probably only being held together by the wallpaper, judged the builder we got in to sort it out.

Thankfully, the Tae Kwon Do training did its stuff and they could both defend themselves very well and didn't get physically damaged in all the squabbles.

They all grew up in their own ways. Daniel was the first to leave the education system. Not just that he was the eldest but also because he wanted to earn money. He got his first job aged 14 collecting golf balls on a driving range in Heaton Mersey. Sometimes he would cycle there, or he went in Mum n Dad's taxi when the weather was inclement.

During his studies at Ridge Danvers College in Cheadle he got a Saturday job at Tittertons Pork Butchers, then as a security guard working for ICTS at Manchester Airport, moving away onto full time in another job after his exams. Not known for his academic achievements, he was however noted as being the class comic and not delivering against his potential. A lot like his Dad.

Born in Stockport - Grew up in the Royal Navy

Danny's role at ICTS was a Profiling Security Agent, responsible for vetting and profiling passengers prior to their travel to the United States. ICTS delivered services to several US based airlines scrutinising their passengers travel credentials, establishing their reason for visit, confirming their identities and ultimately deciding upon their ability to travel. Quite a job for a young man.

Becoming a Royal Marine was Daniels goal and he successfully completed all the entrance exams, physical tests and interview panel. He just needed to attend the Potential Royal Marines Course (PRMC) and received a date for the five-day course when he tore his groin in a Tae Kwon Do tournament and was unable to attend.

The Royal Navy continued to chase him with new dates, month after month but during his rehabilitation period he fell in love with a pretty girl and his head was turned. The Navy kept in contact with him for about nine or ten months after his injury repaired but he didn't attend and therefore never joined up.

Daniel's first full-time job was with First Choice Holidays but only worked there for a few weeks as he had been on a waiting list to start at Stockport Council for Solutions SK as a Control Room Operator, just like his Dad had been.

He also tried to join the police but was not successful. After five years he went to work at Metrolink as a Driver and then he got promoted to Controller, where he continues to deliver tram services safely and efficiently.

When we returned from Australia, Jamie developed a new enthusiasm for reading and studying. His education blossomed and it was such a pleasure to attend parent teacher evenings at school and listen to teachers expound their sentiments on how well he was doing. It was therefore no surprise to find out that he was made Head Boy for his final year at Avondale.

Jamie wanted to be a helicopter pilot in the Army Air Corps and be part of the teams flying Apache's. I went with him to the Army Careers Office in Manchester for a discussion about his military future. The advice he received was good. Take his favourite subjects at College, pass with distinction and do the same at University. Then come back and have some conversations about roles and commitment to HM Government.

The College Jamie wanted to attend was called Aquinas. A Roman Catholic place of education but one that had the best reviews and that is why Jamie wanted to attend. Except the entry rules were quite stringent. First choice was to children in the catchment area. Second was if you are of the Roman Catholic faith. Third if you have a brother or sister already studying there. Then the rest were on a first-come first-served basis. Literally.

Jamie was so determined, he, like many others, camped out overnight in a queue. Jamie was 150th in line, with over two hundred others joining during the early hours of the morning in the queue behind him. When the school opened at 09:00, Jamie went in and got a place. Just like that. A very determined and quite stubborn young man. Just like his Dad.

Jamie successfully applied for a place at the University of Salford and enrolled on the Contemporary Military and International History course. I was with him on the enrolment evening and noted that the lecturers talked about future careers for the successful. Most enter the military as officers, some go into lecturing or museums and some become spies. Right.

Within weeks of starting the course, Jamie wanted to have a chat with me. He had come to the conclusion that he didn't think he could kill anybody and therefore wouldn't be going into HM Armed Forces.

I remember thinking that it was a big decision from a rapidly maturing young man and went with it as it was his choice. I asked him if he wanted to complete his degree and he said yes and so he continued. He got a 2:1 and made his family proud.

Towards the end of the course Jamie interrupted me on the desk top p.c. we had in the front room where I was doing some work, for work on it and said quite casually that the navy's big cheese would be giving a talk to the course that evening back at the University.

It took a bit of rapid-fire Q&A to determine that The First Sea Lord, Rear Admiral Sir Jonathan Band, Commander in Chief Royal Navy and my skipper from the Soberton was indeed presenting a paper at the

University. I had to get a message to him but Jamie said he only had a few minutes.

I rapidly typed a single A4 page, giving my name and address, an explanation of who I was and did he remember me and thanked him for his support when I was in the RN. Banged out in about five minutes. I pressed PRINT, signed it and shoved it into an envelope and wrote Sir Jonathan Band on the envelope, then Jamie disappeared to get his train.

Jamie called me from the University before he returned home. He said how he had found it very difficult to get anywhere near JB as he was thronged by the suited and booted future military officers and stood out in just his shorts and t-shirt wondering how he could deliver my letter he waved in his hand.

It was JB's Aide de Camp (ADC) who was stood to one side and could see Jamie struggling, went over and asked him what the matter was. Jamie said he had a letter from his Dad who used to serve with the Admiral. The ADC did no more than shout for JB's attention and inform him that a son of someone who served with him had a letter for him.

JB didn't read the letter but asked Jamie who his Dad was and as soon as he said Maurice Perkins, JB announced Polly off the Soberton. What a memory. What a man. He gave Jamie some personal time asking him how I was doing and once both had said what they wanted to say, JB turned back to the throng and Jamie made his way home after thanking the ADC. Always good to be polite.

I was still writing up my piece of work on the desktop when the phone rang and Bev shouted that it was for me. I went into the back room and Beverly whispered, "It's the Admiral!"

JB was on a Virgin train heading back down south to London and had called me on his mobile. We spoke for about half an hour and exchanged short versions of how we had got to where we are. I was totally made up that he took the time to listen to my son and engage with him, even more so that he remembered me and talked about our time together on the Soberton.

Born in Stockport - Grew up in the Royal Navy

Through this, my work and my shipmate Smudge the Chef, I have kept in contact with JB over the years. He attended Smudge's fund-raising evening in Goole one evening, accompanied with his ADC and an armed Royal Marine driver. We mustered some of the ships company to attend the presentation he gave and had beers with him back at Smudge's house.

I attended one of his retirement do's, a garden party in Portsmouth Naval Dockyard, at the home of the Commodore there and when he attended Spider's wedding a few years ago. He also commented on a LinkedIn post I made during the Covid-19 pandemic. A top, top man.

Jamie had spells of working as an Assistant Project Manager, a cash-in-transit driver and a tram driver before his vocation and hobby of table-top gaming combined and he is now Game Development Manager for Steamforged Games. A role that suits him and he adores it and came after becoming one of the best table-top gamers in the world.

He was at home and buried in his cave of a bedroom one evening. Bev had called us all into the dining room for tea but Jamie hadn't responded, so jogged upstairs to get his attention. I realised why he couldn't hear us as he had his headphones on and so I raised my voice and said "Jamie, your tea is on the table" and he turned round quickly telling me to hush as he was on a podcast. I retreated backwards, closed the door and went downstairs and told Bev, who asked what a podcast is and my reply didn't help, "How the hell would I know what a podcast is!"

Jamie attended tournaments all over the world and was regularly interviewed on "podcasts" and appears on numerous YouTube videos. He is without doubt, the most famous member of our family. He is also famous in our house for his "Finger of Whisky" moment.

We were sat watching telly and Jamie asked if anyone wanted anything from the kitchen whilst he was going, I was drinking whisky and said can you put some in, "Just a finger" I cautioned. He returned from the kitchen with a tumbler full of whisky and I exclaimed that to drink it would kill me. How could that possibly be a finger, as I demonstrated the horizontal hold with it to indicate half an inch of whisky. Jamie just shrugged and showed is upright finger, indicating about three inches of whiskey. A lesson in language and interpretation was provided forthwith.

Born in Stockport - Grew up in the Royal Navy

Nicola's entry into her first choice College, Aquinas did not require overnight queuing as her brother attended and her application was accepted without fuss. Her budding gymnastics career came to an end following two serious knee injuries but she threw herself into coaching and judging competitions. She is still part of the Stockport School of Gymnastics running competitions and judging in regional ones. She intends to become a national judge and I have no doubt that she will.

Nicola was the first to get married. To Ash, a lovely guy who was still serving in the Army when they met. She went with him and they lived in married quarters in Bulford and Lincoln, before returning to Stockport when Ash made the decision to become a civilian. I was proud as punch to give her away at our local church, St. Matthew's CofE.

By then she had secured a career training to be a paralegal and managed to find gainful employment in Stockport before doing the same in Salisbury and Lincoln, before returning to Stockport. On the way she gave birth to the effervescent Sammy Jay. Samuel James to be formal, or Sam the Tank as our Daniel calls him.

Daniel was the next to trip the light fantastic into marriage when he secured the lovely Sarah. They in turn have created the Two Foot Terrorist (TFT) Jessica and the twins Charlotte and Alexander (aka Destructo), all three are bundles of fun and energy. Just like their Mum and Dad.

Jamie was the last of the trio to enter the formality of marriage and wed Laura. Jamie already had a daughter by then, the lovely Orla and Laura had the charming Louise. Together they created Theo, a wonderful little boy.

At the last count we had seven grandchildren and we get to see most of them every week and all of them on certain occasions like secret garden parties, birthdays and other such events.

Our extended clan includes Mum and Dad, our Ged and his darling wife Jo, nieces Abigail and Olivia. Cousin Babs, niece Georgia, sister-in-law Heather and nephew Thomas. We get together whenever we are able to.

Chapter 28

Becoming an Executive

When we got back from Australia my career began to really blossom and I spent the last 8 years at Metrolink as Operations Director, with increasing budget responsibilities. One of my key successes was driving through change when the Altram PFI failed and Serco working with the client, bought out the remaining shareholders and we took on the revenue risk. We also provided enhanced services at the heart of transport delivery for the 2002 Commonwealth Games held in Manchester, for which I received letters of commendation from the client.

A halcyon period of development for me, for the economic wellbeing of Metrolink and it enabled the client to press ahead with securing support from central government to extend the network. The system has gone from strength to strength ever since.

I wasn't there all the time though, as my bidding expertise was often sought by other colleagues across Serco. I was seconded to Docklands Light Railway (DLR) at the end of 2004 and led the operational solution for our winning bid in 2005 that re-secured the DLR contract for another seven, plus options to extend for two years.

I also supported the initial deployment into Vancouver, Canada for the Richmond Airport Vancouver Project, to extend the Skytrain network and was part of the core team that bid for Edinburgh Tram before being asked to take on the role of bid manager to retain Metrolink. We didn't manage to retain it and I TUPE'd to Stagecoach in the summer of 2007. At that time, I was also working in Dublin, positioning Serco for the Dublin Metro West project that sadly never got off the ground, despite long term engagement with the client. I also provided remote input to the successful tenders for the Dubai Metro. I did have a chance to work there but turned down the opportunity after a five day visit to see what it was like. Dusty, hot, prejudiced and not for me.

Stagecoach made me an offer I couldn't refuse and so I moved on to Atkins as a Client Director for Local Authorities in the Highways & Transportation division, looking after Intelligent Transport Systems. Something very different from what I had done before. Within a short time, I was Operations Director responsible for the northern business unit with over 100 consultants across five different offices.

It was a failing business unit, losing money hand over fist and I turned things round by surrounding myself with like-minded people, changing out some project managers and instilling some simple governance that should have been applied previously. We turned things around and it was another good period of development and taking on a different approach to making money.

The rollercoaster ride hit a wall in 2009 as the world-wide banking crisis really took hold. I carried out the most horrible set of tasks I have ever endured in work over the next eighteen months, to put a lot of people out of work by way of redundancy. I also went from running the northern business to running the whole of ITS nationally within Atkins as our teams shrunk and senior people moved on. It was a very difficult time.

I had been angling for a move into the operational part of the business and away from consultancy as I felt it offered more of a challenge and I could add value but the process was deferred for over a year whilst the consultancy teams were shrunk right down. For a period of time during the change, I worked for 50% in consultancy and 50% in operations. However, when the crunch came, I planted my flag in operations.

Atkins sold the operational part of the business to Skanska in 2013 and I was responsible for managing the TUPE for the midlands area of the business. At the same time, I was part of the core team that won the Peterborough Integrated Highway Services contract as Atkins but it was immediately novated to Skanska on the day we won it.

At the end of 2015 I was asked to support and then to lead the bid for Cambridgeshire Integrated Highways Contract, with a commercial value of £2.1bn as advertised in the Official Journal of the European Union, or OJEU to us. The place where all tenders for the public sector valued over c£1m, must be published.

We submitted our successful Pre-Qualification Questionnaire (PQQ) for Cambridgeshire and it was truly a work of art, consisting of a number of case studies from across our other successful highways contracts. I was going on holiday to the Caribbean the day before submission and worked until late in our Birmingham office but left before the rest of the team. As I was leaving my hilarious colleague Jim, couldn't help but throw out a funny.

He said that he didn't expect to see any photo's of me in my budgie smugglers. A few of the team laughed. I was about to say that I cannot wear budgie smugglers because I am too fat but as I turned round I realised that could upset some of my more rotund colleagues and halfway through the sentence changed the word fat to big.

However, it came out as "I cannot wear budgie smugglers because I am too big" which was probably the worst thing I could have said as everyone roared laughing or shouting at me to stop boasting. It didn't matter what I said, they wouldn't have it.

So, when we arrived in port and I found a stall selling embossed t-shirts, I just had to have one, got a photo and messaged it to Jim. We still laugh about it today.

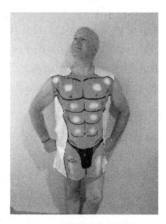

Going into 2016, I had a lot on my plate.

Chapter Twenty

Mental Health and Well-being

Born in Stockport - Grew up in the Royal Navy

I am going to try and explain the three things that challenged my mental health and well-being. One caught me by surprise, one arguably I should have known about and the third was pre-planned and premeditated.

There is no doubt in my mind that 2016 was incredibly busy year for me. Leading the bid for Cambridgeshire was a massive hurdle. The client deployed an untried process and there was evidence of unfairness that raised objections. The client responded by swapping out staff and tried to persevere with an amended version of the procurement process but that too foundered and a third was deployed after lengthy delays.

The procurement was via competitive dialogue. A resource hungry, time consuming series of events, spread over many months. The procurement process that had commenced in the Autumn of 2015 was not completed until the Spring of 2017. I spent most of my working weeks in and around Cambridge and away from home.

At the same time, the football club had been fighting a takeover assault from our rugby club partners at Didsbury Sports Ground that erupted once both clubs had contributed to the £1m+ project to build ten new changing rooms and completely re-furbish the clubhouse, adding a second bar and constructing a brand-new state of the art kitchen and café. The rugby club had threatened legal action, entered into a complicated series of meetings and exchange of correspondence.

Our clubhouse is built on land leased from a charity that forms part of the River Mersey flood protection measures. Flood Basin No.1 is the title used by the Environment Agency, or Simon Field as the Covenant left by the great Henry Simon dictates. The rugby and football clubs have equal shares in Didsbury Sports Ground, the company limited by guarantee that runs the sporting facilities. It was this shareholding that the rugby club wanted to alter.

The EA wanted to raise the level of the flood basin above the floor level of the clubhouse and offered compensation. After two years of negotiations by a combined team of both rugby and football club officers, we had secured £265,000 compensation from the EA and added £35,000 jointly between both clubs. I then used that to secure £300,000 grant from the FA and the rugby guys got £100,000 grant from the RFU, plus another

£100,000 as a loan. Together we secured another £250,000 from the English & Welsh Cricket Board and Sport England.

I was chair of Didsbury Sports Ground and Didsbury Playing Fields Association, a charity we set up to manage the portfolio of facilities and be the vehicle to manage the grants etc. and attended almost every single meeting.

I spent a lot of time gathering legal support from the Football Association and from within the ranks of the playing and officer membership. Once I had all that in place, I led the fightback and indicated that we were ready to go to court.

The rugby club baulked at that and had probably assumed we would roll over but we didn't. We just needed time to get our act in gear.

The challenge diverted attention from leveraging additional income from our new facilities by way of external events such as weddings, birthday and anniversary parties, etc. and keeping all our creditors happy.

I was also managing the veteran over 35's as a fourth team on a Saturday afternoon.

Towards the end of 2016, Skanska lost out on the re-tendering of one of our Highways England Area contracts in the south west that resulted in one of my team's future put into question and a raft of individuals from the team were put onto a TUPE list. My team were based down in Ipswich. Geographically distanced from both their main work area in the south west and me. At least I could "pop down" to Ipswich from Cambridge.

My Central Control team in Birmingham were having staff retention problems and a lot of my time was taken up in Birmingham as well. Again, just a jaunt along the A14 just as the big road widening scheme got underway and there were tens of miles of speed restrictions and lane closures. Brilliant.

Nicola, my daughter, was having a difficult pregnancy as was my daughter in law, so there were some family emotional issues to manage as well.

Born in Stockport - Grew up in the Royal Navy

Just before Christmas I was asked if I wanted to lead the Skanska regional growth team in Manchester and jumped at the chance to work more locally. So, a soft start in December, with a roll-out of the team to begin once the Cambridgeshire Bid was submitted.

The weeks before Christmas were ugly in terms of time. The whole bid core team was running out of the Birmingham office and we went into an intense 15 to 20 hours a day burn in the final week before submission. Hectic does not cover it sufficiently. It was mad.

I had also put a counter proposal to the rugby club and reached a compromise agreement with them in between Christmas and New Year, which has largely held, up to the point of capturing these stories in a book.

We got the nod that we had won the Cambridgeshire Highways business but had to keep quiet as the client needed to go through a legal lockdown subject to any challenges by the losing party, which they did.

Sammy Jay was born on 8th January and Theodore was born on 16th March 2017.

All was well and dandy. I was in Manchester city centre attending a low-key CBI round-table event on regional devolution and its impact on Greater Manchester. Just as the meeting started, I felt ill. I thought I was going to be sick, then I felt dizzy and realising what I thought were the symptoms of a faint, decided to push the chair backwards and go lie on the floor, pull my knees up a bit and went to sleep. At least that is what I thought I did.

I woke up about 8 or 9 hours later in a hospital bed with Beverly sat beside me and doctor stood over me and was really confused. I asked where I was and Bev said that she had already answered that question a hundred times. I asked her again and she said that we were in Manchester Royal Infirmary. I wanted to know what had happened. Bev again said that she had answered that question multiple times as well.

I begged her to humour me and so she said that I had a funny turn. What?

Born in Stockport - Grew up in the Royal Navy

The doctor then said, I think he is coming round. Let's ask him some questions. He asked me to unlock my mobile phone that Bev was holding. I didn't know the number. He asked me who I worked for and I replied Atkins. Bev shook her head and said, you work for Skanska and haven't worked for Atkins for about 5 years. I thought, of course I do, why would I say Atkins.

The doctor asked me if I had any grandchildren and I said yes. He asked how many. I said one. Bev shook her head. Three, I asked? Bev shook her head and said no, we have five. I thought of course we have five, why the hell did I say three, why did I even say one. It was confusing.

The doctor advised me that he thought I had Global Transient Amnesia. A complete loss of memory and the brain is unable to retain any information for the duration of the attack and I hadn't been asleep as I first thought.

What had happened was I had experienced a sudden and overwhelming rise in my blood pressure. So high that it went off the scale. I hadn't lain down on the floor. I had stood up, packed my bag, picked up my coat and walked out of the CBI meeting.

The lady leading the briefing followed me out as she thought my behaviour was odd. I was walking around in the reception outside but she noticed that I was very pale and suggested I sat down and have a glass of water.

Not satisfied with my condition, she and another member of the discussion group, walked me out of the building with the intention of going to a NHS blood donor office in the next building for some advice and help. We never got there. I collapsed in the street and they dialled 999 for an ambulance.

I do have some snapshot memories of that day but they are so fleeting, it is difficult to know if it is my memory or something someone has told me.

A paramedic opening the buttons on my shirt to attach some electrodes and apologising for having to roughly shave my chest, whilst "Blues & Twooh's" were the background and I apologised to him. Being lay down in an MRI scanner and lay on a gurney in a corridor looking at the upside-down face of a lady patient in a gurney going the other way. Then I woke up in a bed with Bev next to me and I started asking questions.

Other than that, I have almost no memory of the day and my long-term memory was seriously distorted for months and months. Lots of things that I should have known but I could not remember. The neurologist called it "data retrieval errors" like I was a bloody computer. It took time for things to settle down. What was worst was the constant migraines and vertigo that ran 24/7 for about five or six weeks. It was very debilitating.

I saw the neurologist consultant several times, over a number of weeks and he was really pleased that he had a case study with a live patient, as normally most people who experience such a high blood pressure die of a stroke or a heart attack. He had a complete record, as the lady from the CBI accompanied me to hospital and handed over to Beverly. Both of whom confirmed that I never fell asleep, I just kept asking the same questions over and over again. What has happened and where am I?

All the post event medical checks and subsequent MRI scans confirmed that my vital organs were in good condition. My brain gave out much like a fuse does when an appliance is overloaded. That is the best explanation I have. The neurologist also said that I should not try to remember as I won't be able to. It's just a blank. He also said that my memory would return and it has.

Medication got the migraines under control and then it was a long fight to regain my fitness. It shocked me how much the event and convalescence had taken out of me. I had firmly believed I was mentally indestructible, but this has proved otherwise.

I had to clear myself of everything. Work, football and DSG / DPFA stuff.

Skanska were terrific with me and helped with my recovery immensely. As an organisation but more so as work colleagues asked after me and gave me lots of support. In time, I was able to talk quite openly about it and wanted to do so, in order to help others.

I did state earlier that arguably I should have known that it was coming as my family and friends all commented that I was getting angry and frustrated with the slightest thing. Though some mentioned it and I ignored them, most did not speak to me about it.

One of my key messages to help people, whether they are family, friends or work colleagues, if you see their behaviour alter, sit them down and have a chat. If that is not the right moment, find another time when you can take a moment to find out what is going on. It could help prevent someone else falling into the same trap I did.

I got back to work later in 2017 with a phased return programme. However, the whole thing had shaken my resolve and I investigated what my status was with my pension arrangements and took some advice.

As we got into the spring of 2018 I had made the decision that I was going to retire early, I just didn't know when. I let my boss know and he suggested I hang on a few more months as the business would be re-organising and there is will likely be redundancies. We can then have the discussion again. The following day I picked up a really bad water infection.

My GP, Dr Alexander Bayes wasn't happy with some of my PSA readings and referred me to the Urology Clinic, where after some more tests was diagnosed with prostate cancer. This was the one that caught me by surprise.

By then, I had made the decision to retire and left Skanska as a full-time employee at the end of the calendar year of 2018, so the cancer treatment was a distraction.

I elected to have Brachytherapy. Essentially a bunch of radioactive tiny bullets, the size of rice grains, injected into my prostate. I likened them to Homer Simpsons glowing green isotopes. They remained active for about eighteen months before becoming inert. They are still in there. I have got used to the side effects and manage them quite effectively now.

Prior to that, I had a challenge to lead and deliver a highway industry event for Skanska's clients and supply chain partners down in Somerset. I had fantastic support from a small team of clever people. I had to engage with a number of our supply chain partners, consultants, technical specialists etc. over a short period of time.

Born in Stockport - Grew up in the Royal Navy

It was whilst working with former colleagues at Atkins, one our consultant partners that I was in a conversation with a senior chap called Alex, whom I believed I hadn't met. He had mentioned that he thought he had met me the previous year at a CBI event in Manchester. I had to apologise and say that I couldn't remember anything about the day as I had a funny turn that led to me losing any memory of the day after I collapsed. He said yes, he knew, he helped put me into the recovery position whilst waiting for the ambulance..... I got to meet him in person at the event, shook his hand and thanked him for his help that day. What a small world.

The pre-planned and premeditated thing was retirement itself.

I chose the end of year as it was also Skanska's financial year and therefore maximised my company bonus and employee share options. Both of which tipped up nice cash amounts in the Spring and Summer of 2019.

However, I had not adequately prepared myself for doing nothing. I know that sounds strange but I had gone from a senior position (Technical Services Director) responsible for around 75 staff in two teams located in Birmingham and Ipswich, as well as providing technical leadership to around 250 professional staff across the various contracts within Infrastructure Services. I was used to providing input to bids, was part of the division's senior management team and constantly on the phone, attending meetings, sharing knowledge and promoting good practice. To go from all that to literally doing nothing is quite a profound thing.

Beverly told me off for trying to run our new retired life in line with some sort of programme of activity. She told me to stop putting things in the diary for the both of us.

I got quite tense and very irritable. Shades of 2016 and 2017 and it took me until summer of 2019 to properly settle down into doing nothing. Every day is a Sunday kind of mentality.

Skanska asked me to continue with a couple of projects, one with Infrastructure Services down in Somerset and to help Cementation with their business development and strategic planning. We formed a little company for both Bev and me to carry out part time, ad-hoc work. Bev for Stockport School of Gymnastics and me for Skanska, Serco and Dyer &

Butler. It took us up to the lockdown for COVID-19 when everything came to a halt.

Another factor that has hit me hard is losing friends. Particularly friends who have served in HM Armed Forces. Ex-services people have an affinity. At some point in our lives, we signed up for Queen and Country to decide how best to use us. We all contributed to the defence of the realm and it remains a bond throughout our lives. However, that contribution was put to the test.

Mick Brown, ex-Army and good friend at Metrolink in November 2018, went after a long battle with stomach cancer. The turnout from the family from Metrolink and his own family was enormous. I lived with Mick for five weeks when we worked in Brussels and did all our tram driver training together. He wouldn't get out of bed until I had flattened all the cockroaches and made him a cup of tea. He was my friend.

Bernard Chase ex-Royal Marine slipped away after losing his fight against throat cancer. I and some other friends managed to get a drink with him in the pub a few weeks before his watch was over. I couldn't make the funeral as we were away on holiday. We reminisced on Metrolink days and our wonderful weekend stag do's to Dublin, when Bernard demonstrated he was Roy Cropper's stunt double.

Then in the summer we lost "H", ex-Royal Navy and a shipmate off HMS Antrim. Martin Harrison, or Harry to us. "H" had a series of strokes that hit him badly. It was in the post stroke evaluation that the doctors found his body riddled with tumours and that is what had caused the strokes. He slipped away fairly rapidly after that. Flash to bang was no more than seven weeks. I read out a eulogy with Smaff at the funeral and we tipped a fair few beer's in his memory at the family wake and our own mess wake, including some horrible black stuff that Harry made us drink at one of the 2E Mess Northern Monkey's reunions. Harry was one of the funniest blokes I have ever met.

Pete Ford finally succumbed to the terrible lung disease that had plagued him since he left the RAF. My oldest friend and it was just as difficult a funeral as the others. I cried several times from knowing he had gone, right through to the funeral. We all sang "You go your way and I'll go mine" in his memory and I cried again, as I did as I first typed up this part of my story. A very funny man and author of so many memories and escapades. Once met, never forgotten..

It was the realisation that we are mere mortals and we need to make the most of every day that probably brought me down to earth.

Postscript

Since retirement, I have returned to working as a volunteer with the Sports Ground Charity, the operating company that manages the facilities and my football club. I am trying my best not to take on too much but do devote effort into engaging with the community around us, to try and make better use of the fabulous facilities we have created.

I also try to spend as much time with our wonderful grandchildren as Beverly provides childcare for five of the seven, for four days a week as professional child-care costs are extortionate and we help to reduce that. We also get the bonus of handing them back to their parents when they are tired or broken.

Spending time with my friends is also especially important for me and I keep in contact with a lot of lads from my first ship HMS Antrim. We have a self-help group and do our best to look after each other as various trials and tribulations test different individuals from time to time. We are immensely relaxed in each other's company and chill over beers whenever we can. We also have an annual reunion, usually in Portsmouth that attracts a wider crowd of similar thinking people.

Social media is a great help. I use Facebook, WhatsApp, Messenger and the phone to keep in contact with a wide group of friends, both ex-services and from where I used to work.

Looking back on my career, I have made some significant contributions to the Royal Navy, the Local Authority in Stockport, to Metrolink and transport in general, to Highways Maintenance and Construction along with Rail. The voluntary work I have done to grow the game of football has been an immense challenge and it is not over yet.

I don't think I have done too bad for a kid off a tough council estate, who left school with no qualifications.....

Printed in Great Britain
by Amazon